Thriving With Hair Loss

Helping women look younger, feel more confident, and be more secure

By
Peggy Knight

*Wig mentor, designer, and founder
of Locks of Love*

Published by
Hybrid Global Publishing
333 E 14th Street
#3C
New York, NY 10003

Manufactured in the United States of America, or in the United Kingdom when distributed elsewhere.

Knight, Peggy.
Thriving With Hair Loss
    ISBN: 978-1-961757-07-3
    eBook: 978-1-961757-08-0
    LCCN: 2023916619

Cover design by: Julia Kuris
Copyediting by: Wendie Pecharsky
Interior design by: Suba Murugan
Author photo by: SF Chronicle

www.peggyknight.com

*I dedicate this book to my oldest and dearest friend,
Kathy Hale. Kathy held me up when I was down and reveled
in my successes. She was the inspiration behind the charity
"Locks of Love." She is and has always been
my support system.*

CONTENTS

INTRODUCTION – MY STORY

I share my personal story and experience with hair loss, which happened when I was 14. I watched in horror as the first strand of hair fell to the floor. The slow shedding soon gave way to rapid hair loss, leaving me looking like a dog with mange.

Finding that first spot is devastating for a young girl, or anyone for that matter.

At the tender age of 14, I learned more about alopecia areata than any teenage girl needs to know. As the condition grabbed hold of my life, squeezed it, twisted it, and spat it out, I was left to find my own way. After 60 years of dealing with this medical hair loss condition, I am now here to share my story with you. You will read about the emotions I experienced, the coping methods I developed, and the solutions I created. You will read about how it felt, from the discovery of the first falling strand to the loss of all body hair.

The emotions I describe are not unique to me. They are shared by almost anyone who suffers from the shock of medical hair loss. No one is exempt from the emotional roller coaster that this life-altering condition brings. By sharing my experience with you, it is my hope that you won't feel alone. Many thousands of men, women, and children have traveled this road before us. I have walked the path, blazed the trail, and cleared the way so you can have an easier journey. I am here to tell you about the ups and downs of the journey and let you know there is life after hair loss.

My story spans over six decades, covering all the stages of loss. Today, I have beautiful, shiny, youthful hair that stays put without the use of tape or glue, thanks to my beautiful new hairpiece. My dream came full circle as I sat in the salon chair only days after receiving my new hair. ***New hair, new me.***

After facing the trauma of hair loss myself, I have dedicated my life to helping women experiencing hair loss. I've walked in your shoes and know your pain. Let me guide you through the maze to help you find your own way. My goal in writing this book is to empower and educate women to know their options and to feel whole and beautiful again. I don't want you to walk away feeling doomed by hair loss. It is a completely unpredictable condition–and I have known many clients who have regrown their hair. We are thrilled when this happens because regrowth is a major cause for celebration. Whether you have thinning hair, chemotherapy-induced loss, self-inflicted loss, or alopecia areata hair loss, this book is for you.

In an effort to help myself and others, in 1982, I founded the Image Center for Women in San Francisco, where we focused on helping women regain their self-esteem and return to a normal, active lifestyle after experiencing changes in their physical appearance due to hair loss.

The institute started when I met the founder of Victoria's Secret. He became my partner, and together, we created the concept. Our vision was to incorporate necessity and beauty, much the way he created Victoria's Secret. We soon became the talk of the hair replacement industry and had visitors from around the country. With my knowledge of hair replacement and his understanding of what women want and need, we made a dynamic team. We offered hair replacement, makeup, scarves, lingerie, and breast prostheses to our clients. The salon was always filled with women having an initial cut or getting their hair coiffed for a big event. I learned so much about marketing and customer service from the master himself. He was truly a brilliant partner, and I credit much of my success to him. His approach was to treat the woman from the inside out. Heal the fear and provide the best solution to her situation. He was adamant about conquering the ups and downs of somebody's life and watching them thrive as a result.

Our union morphed into a network of 15 sales representatives across the US and abroad. My institute also nurtured the development of high-quality hairpieces and wigs through Peggy Knight Wigs. Some of our clients are still here with us today. Recently, I worked with my client, Alanna Powell, the founder of Boldly Me Academy, an online educational program that provides the tools people need to improve social and behavioral health, build self-esteem, develop coping mechanisms for life's challenges, and empower themselves to live their lives to their fullest unique potential. We first met when she was 14 years old, and now she has three children going to college. That, my friends, is what I call loyalty. So many of my long-time clients continue with me because of the quality of hair and customer service. I am honored to have such a loyal client following.

In the book, I'll share how the internet does not always provide accurate information when it comes to wigs. Just because you read it on the internet does not mean it is true! Education is crucial when working with something so emotional and cosmetic as a woman's hair. I traveled the world visiting wig manufacturers to educate myself and my clients.

Today, as founder and president of Peggy Knight Wigs, I oversee the research and development of a full product line of wigs and custom hairpieces created specifically for girls, teens, and women with medical hair loss. I am committed to creating hair prostheses that enable everyone experiencing hair loss to lead a normal life, a worry-free walk in the wind, or while playing sports.

This comprehensive guide will help you cope with hair loss and find solutions for moving forward, whether your hair loss is temporary or permanent, and give you the courage and inspiration to keep searching for a solution that is right for you.

Finding the perfect hair solutions for you is not walking into a wig shop and trying on wigs. The process is much more involved. We take into consideration all of your personal needs. I am happy to share with you what I've learned while designing signature wigs for over 40 years. Let me take you by the hand and guide you to your perfect hair. Remember, you are in the driver's seat of your life. You get to choose your wig. All you need is guidance. Let me be your hair loss guide.

CHAPTER 1

GOING, GOING, GONE!

Hair loss was not in my realm of consideration. No child should have to be tested with such a loss.

I've traveled a long, tough road to get to this place in my life. I learned about hair loss at the age when other girls were exploring hairstyles.

Losing one's hair is never easy, a fact that millions know all too well. But it's devastating when you're a youngster who's enthralled with hair. As a girl and then a young teen, my dark, curly hair—a byproduct of my Italian heritage—was not only my pride and joy, it was my obsession. At age 10, I made what could very well have been the world's very first highlight by creating a tiny fall out of silvery thread, attaching it to a bobby pin, and then blending it in with my own hair.

During the next few years, my girlfriends and I would spend hours in front of the mirror experimenting with new 'dos. My dad would pound on the bathroom door, saying, "Hurry up, girls, you've been in there for hours!" He was right – but after all, we were fussing over our hair, and that was just *what girls did*. Great hair made us feel, well, great. Conversely, of course, bad hair days made us feel terrible – and not just about our hair. I learned about the lack of self-esteem at an early age. It took years to overcome.

I remember vividly the day my mother gave me a home permanent wave right before my First Holy Communion. She meant well, but the result was the perm from hell! Nothing could calm down the frizz, and I was sure that my life was ruined forever. As all of my girlfriends were leaving home in their white dresses and veils the following morning, I curled up on my bed and sobbed. I hated my hair and wanted to hide away forever. Instead, my parents sent me off to church to face the humiliation. I'm pretty sure that I burned all of the photos of that holy day. As I look back on that hair-related incident that once seemed to be the end of the world, I realize that the perm was a subtle preparation for what lay ahead. The day would come when I would long for even those frizzy locks I once hated.

What was happening?

As I brushed my hair in preparation for my 14th birthday party, I felt a smooth patch on the side of my head. Where was the hair that was supposed to be there? In a panic, I ran into the living room to show my parents. "What happened? What happened?" I cried. "Look at my hair!"

The round bald spot was the size of a quarter. I didn't know what had caused it, but I knew something was very wrong. Finding that first spot is devastating to a young girl. I sat down and cried. Despite their alarm, my parents decided to give my hair time to re-grow before rushing me to the doctor. That seemed like a good call because, in a short period of time, fuzz covered the smooth surface. All was forgotten... until a second spot appeared on the other side of my head. And then another, and another. The spots seemed to have a life of their own. As one began sprouting new hair and filling in, another grew even larger and balder.

Thus began a cruel yo-yo process of having my hair grow in and fall out and grow in and fall out. It would actually have been easier if my hair had all fallen out immediately. If it was going to come out, let it come out. If it was going to grow in, let it grow in. But no: every day was a different story. Eventually, the spots started to appear more and more frequently. So instead of one spot on the side of my head, there would be two that would grow to the point where they merged together to form a figure eight.

Eventually, it became clear that my hair was falling out faster than it was growing in. By the age of 24, *I was completely bald.*

When I started to lose my hair, my first experience seeing a medical doctor seemed like the end of the world. I felt hopeless and as if I were doomed to be bald forever. Looking back on my own experience has given me the perspective to help countless women experiencing hair loss.

Shortly after I had lost my first patch of hair, my petite, beautiful mother developed a bald spot of her own, which simply grew larger as others developed. Within six months, she had lost all of her waist-long hair, along with all the rest of the hair on her body. Questions began to race through my mind: *Is this what I have to look forward to? What could have caused this hair loss? Do I have a strange disease that I share with my mother? Is our nutrition lacking, or are we using the wrong shampoo?*

Fear of exposure

As a teenager with hair loss, my primary concern quickly became hiding my increasingly bare head from the rest of the world. I had no idea how to cover up the four-inch-diameter bald spot on the top of my head, along with the others that had cropped up, for school picture day. I took mental notes as our local hair stylist somehow managed to create something out of nothing. Before long, all of the spots had been camouflaged, and I was ready for my close-up. The artfully created look might have been unusual, but at least I didn't look hairless.

The difficult task of cosmetically concealing my growing baldness took longer and longer as I had less and less hair to work with. I would spend huge amounts of time teasing my remaining hair and using hairspray to hold the style in place. The night of my senior prom, I was supposed to be picked up at 6:30 p.m. for dinner, but as the afternoon turned to evening, my hairstyle was still a work in progress. This time, I was forced to add a hairpiece, which I attached to my remaining hair with dozens of bobby pins. The fake hair blended with my own, but my entire head was so heavily doused with hairspray that it had a lacquered finish. With just 30 minutes left on the clock, I finally completed my updo (and I use the word literally) and had just enough time to slip on my dress and make up my face. At the prom, I had to walk —and dance — like I had a book on my head because, with the slightest tip, the entire coif tilted. But I made it! That wouldn't always be the case.

Wearing scarves and hats

As my hair loss progressed, first eyebrow pencil and then scalp crayons and hair additions were incorporated into my routine. I longed for those days when I was able to get up, wash my hair and run out the door. What used to take five minutes – unless I was fooling around with hairstyles – now routinely took about an hour from start to finish, with much of that time spent in frustration and tears.

Eventually, things got to the point where my hair was so thin that I couldn't cover the bald spots with my hair. By high school, I had already started wearing scarves to cover the missing patches of hair, and they became my trademark. Each scarf matched the outfit of the day: not difficult because my mother or I made most of my clothes. Unfortunately, the school had a dress code that prohibited head coverings. The principal and most of the teachers knew about my situation, so my scarves were approved. On one occasion, however, I was confronted by a substitute teacher who ordered me to remove my scarf in front of the entire class. Profoundly humiliated, I bolted out of the classroom and headed home. That afternoon, my parents visited the school, and the teacher apologized to me the next day. The gesture, however well-intentioned, could not erase the pain and embarrassment that I suffered.

Scarves quickly became a mainstay of my wardrobe at home and on the road. I had one in every color and material. They were stashed in my purse, glove compartment, next to the bed, in my gym bag, and in my suitcase. All the while, I never knew when a big wind might blow, leaving me bareheaded.

Hats were also a good cover-up for bald spots, and they prevented the wind from totally devastating a hairstyle that took me hours to create. Accordingly, I made sure to have one for every occasion: casual hats, sports hats, and dress hats in all colors, styles, and fabrics. My style efforts, however, did nothing to stem the lack of self-esteem caused by my hair loss.

CHAPTER 2

SEARCHING FOR A CURE

There had to be a better way. However, my search for a way to stop my hair loss got out of control and that prompted me to find a solution—rather than a cure—for hair loss.

Like so many of my clients, inadequate hair replacement solutions forced compromises in every aspect of my life. Eventually, I just stopped living a good part of my life.

To this day, nearly 60 years later, we still have no known cause or cure.

As my mother's hair was already falling out when I started losing mine, we both were looking for a cure, not temporary solutions to our hair loss. Our search for a cure started with a visit to our family physician and lasted for almost 10 years. We were sure that our hair loss could be easily explained and certain that the doctor would just prescribe a pill to stop the hair loss. Much to our surprise and horror, he knew we had alopecia areata but didn't know the cause or cure.

Our doctor told us that our condition was thought to be caused by stress. We had no idea what he meant by this. I had nothing to be stressed about except the bald spots that were growing in size on my head. He was partially right: The more hair I lost, the more stress I felt. Still, the question remained: Which came first, the stress or the baldness? This was honestly the lowest point of my alopecia journey. But there's more to come.

We were referred to a San Francisco dermatologist, Dr. Vera Price, medical advisor of the National Alopecia Areata Foundation (NAAF). (Note that I was a founding member of NAAF.) We were convinced that a specialist in alopecia areata would have the answer, so off to the city we went. I remember crying my heart out during the ride. I felt so alone and isolated. No one, not even my family, could understand what I was going through. The tears came from a place in the pit of my stomach, so deep I felt like I could die.

The dermatologist explained that it is quite rare for two members of the same family to be afflicted with alopecia areata. While this was interesting information, all we wanted to know was how to cure this strange disease. Although quite knowledgeable about the condition, the dermatologist did not have a cure for us. It was too hard to imagine, especially at the age of 14, that a condition existed for which a doctor could not provide a cure.

Another desperate attempt for a cure

Our family hairstylist offered us her idea for a cure: an ultraviolet rake. When it was plugged in, it was lavender, smelled like burning electricity, and made the sound of a bug zapper. I was not sure what this device was supposed to do for me, but everyone believed it would stimulate hair growth. I sat for hours under the machine, praying that it would work, but my hair continued to fall out.

Cortisone creams were the next course of treatment. We applied it twice a day to the scalp, which also meant I had to wash my hair twice a day. With each washing, I watched in despair as more of my remaining hair trickled down the drain. To this day, I am unable to look into a drain without feeling the ache from those early years of my hair loss. I can't tell you if the cortisone cream worked, but I can tell you that I was glad to see it go. I looked and felt greasy, and the creams left a mess on my towels and pillow-cases.

As my hair loss accelerated, the doctors started me on a series of cortisone shots that were administered directly into the scalp. These painful monthly shots kept the alopecia at bay, at least for a while. As I wanted to maintain my hair for as long as possible, I became a cortisone junkie. Let me explain. Back in the 1960s and early 70s, there were no electronic medical records, so I would go from doctor to doctor to get more cortisone to slow down the hair loss. But it came at a cost, as too much cortisone can have adverse effects. But it was like a drug; I had to find a way to get more.

As the spots grew in size, though, the number of shots increased, and soon the doctor was using multiple needles. Each shot had five needles attached to it. One time I had 100 shots in my head during one session. Think about how barbaric this was. I would leave the medical facility and drive home in tears because of what I had just endured. While I didn't complain about the pain to others, I do recall feeling very sorry for myself. The pain was unbearable and left me with excruciating headaches. But yet again, there was no regrowth.

Soon the shots stopped working as well, so I graduated to intralesional corticosteroid injections. For many years I took these treatments hoping for a complete cure. They did slow down the loss for a while, but my hair never grew back completely. I was playing cortisone roulette. I went from one doctor to another like a junkie. At one point, a doctor had the sense to figure out my game and cut me off, explaining the dangers of prolonged cortisone steroid use. But I didn't care about the long-term effects. I only cared about regrowth. I desperately wanted *hair*, and if it meant taking a drug that might be harmful to me in the future, then so be it. This program failed me as well.

My next visit was to an endocrinologist to have my thyroid tested. It turned out that I did have an underactive thyroid, so the doctor prescribed medication. I thought I had finally found the answer and was sure that my hair would start growing back any day. I waited and waited… for regrowth that never happened.

Holy sutures

I thought I had found the holy grail of answers. A wig sutured to my head was the biggest headache of my alopecia journey.

One day while in Hawaii, my home for 10 years, I saw a commercial for a permanent solution to baldness. A man wearing a toupee dove into the pool, swam across, came out, and shook his wet hair.

It didn't move! I found out later that he had his hair sutured to his head.

This was my answer! If I had my hair permanently attached to my head with sutures, my wig would not fly off in the Hawaiian Tradewinds, and surely, I would be secure at last. Off I marched to see the doctor, and days later, I was prepped for surgery. Long-running stitches around the perimeter of my head were used as an attachment for my wig. It was days before the headache subsided. Each and every suture entry and exit point was swollen and painful. The infection from the wig bacteria took literally years to heal. I was too embarrassed to go to see a doctor for fear of exposing my secret: **I was bald!**

After enduring this misery for several years, I noticed my wig was turning red in color. Again, too embarrassed to see a trained stylist or colorist, I decided to dye it myself. (Please brace your-self, gentle reader: this part of the story is not pretty.)

I bought a box of Lady Clairol, read the instructions, and headed for the shower. The second the peroxide hit my open oozing sutures, the excruciating pain began. I slumped down in the shower, crying and wishing I would die. My best friend picked me up and took me to the emergency room, where an ER doctor looked at me in horror. His exact words were: "Who did this to you? You are lucky this infection did not go into your brain."

As the doctor removed my sutures, I cried, not only from the overwhelming pain but because it felt as though my security was being cut away. To this day, almost 50 years later, I still have scars on my head from those sutures.

The birth of my mission

This harrowing experience is what catapulted me into the world of wigs. If I was so desperate to have hair that would not blow off my head that I was prepared to undergo such massive risk and pain, I was not alone. After 40 years of working with women with hair loss, I have learned that there are only two things important to them:

1. Security
2. A natural look

In my attempt to have both natural looking hair and have it secured properly to my head, I almost lost my life. I vowed at that time that no one should *ever* have to go through what I did to have hair. As a result of this vow, my first company was born: Knight and Day Hair Products.

CHAPTER 3

WHAT KIND OF WIG IS RIGHT FOR ME? (HOW TO SHOP FOR A WIG AND CARE FOR IT)

Today, wigs are available in a wide range of styles, materials, and colors. Knowing how to shop for a wig and care for it is essential for making the most of your purchase. In this chapter, I will provide you with tips and tricks on how to choose the perfect wig for you, how to care for it properly, and how to store it to ensure its longevity. From synthetic wigs to human hair wigs, I've got you covered!

How to shop for a wig

There are four tips to keep in mind when shopping for a wig.

1. First, decide what style of wig you want. There are wigs for all occasions, from everyday wear to special occasions.
2. Next, consider the color of the wig. Do you want to match your natural hair color or try a new color?
3. Then, consider the base, size, hair length, and hair type you want.

4. Finally, think about how much you want to spend. Wigs range in price from under $500 to $5,000 and more.

1. Wig style

Just like when you are building a house, you are going to want a solid foundation as you build it. When it comes to wigs, consider the cap first. There are different caps for different situations. First, think about how much hair you have. Some caps are designed to fit best over hair versus a bald scalp.

A wig with a one-size-fits-all cap will have more give to it. Therefore, it can stretch over your full head of hair, then fit snuggly your head. Wigs with this type of cap are good for before, during, and after chemotherapy.

You need to answer a lot of questions prior to deciding on a wig. These include:

- What caused your hair loss?
- How long do you expect to have hair loss?
- What is your activity level? For example, if you are a runner and want to wear your wig, just buy a cheap wig for running.
- Do you consider yourself more feminine, or do you identify more as a tomboy?
- What size wig do you need? Wigs come in all sizes, from petite to large.
- What is your age group? A child's wig is less dense than an adult wig.
- Is the wig you purchase returnable?
- Does your wig require styling?

2. Consider your wig's color

In my experience, I've seen a lot of people wearing wigs that are the wrong color. The reason? It doesn't match their skin tone. In fact, they don't know how to match their skin tone. Always match your wig to *unexposed* skin on your body. For example, match it to the skin under your arm. The problem is that many people want to go back to a wig color they had in the past, and after we go through skin tone analysis, they often say, "I can't believe I've been wearing that color wig. It's totally the wrong color." If they have a wig they like but is the wrong color, it can be colored if it's human hair. They don't need to throw it away! Most human hair wigs need to have the color refreshed every 12-18 months anyway due to color oxidation.

3. Length and style of the wig

Most people with alopecia or any type of long-term hair loss never change their hairstyle. And most of the time, their hair is oxidized beyond what it should be. So, to make them more comfortable, I take them through some visualization exercises so we can come up with the right look for them. Here's what a typical session might look like: I call this the "braille method." I ask them, "If you had hair on your head today, what would it look like?" Often, they try to describe it but can't find the words. I ask them to close their eyes and visualize their natural hair growing on their head. A hundred percent of the time, they tell me what length it would be, whether there would be bangs, and if their hair would be straight or curly. They give me a detailed explanation of what it would look like, which tells me they know what they want. What I love about this exercise is that they realize they don't have to look like a mannequin in a wig shop. They have control over what they want their hair to look like. It's empowering.

Tip: Hire a professional to color your wig. Most wigs should be colored every 12 to 18 months. They can also be highlighted. *Never color your own wig.* Keep in mind that all hair has had some processing, whether by the sun or by hair coloring. Less expensive human hair has been processed more. There's really no such thing as "virgin wig." Experienced stylists will want to know the source of the hair and will test a strand before coloring. If you care for your wig properly, your wig should last for years.

4. Price of wigs

As noted, wig prices vary widely from under $500 to thousands of dollars. When you've decided on the style, color, and price of the wig you want, you can start shopping around. You can look for wigs online or in stores. If you're buying a wig online, be sure to read the reviews before you purchase. And if you're buying a wig in a store, be sure to try it on before you buy it. And you always want to ask upfront, "What is the return policy?"

How do I take care of my wig?

All wigs require regular home care. This generally involves shampooing and conditioning. Most wigs come with general care instructions, which should be followed for optimal results. **[insert QR code for Wash Video]**

How often should I wash my wig?

A good rule of thumb is to wash your wig every seven to 10 days, and if you wear your wig infrequently, I recommend it every two weeks. To determine when your wig needs to be washed, shake your head, and if it flows freely, there's no need to wash your hair. However, if when you move your head, the hair clumps, it's time to wash your wig. How does your wig get dirty? From the environment! And if you are a smoker or are in an environment where others are smoking, your wig will pick that up like a magnet.

If you have thinning hair on your head, the oils on your scalp will absorb into your own hair. If you have no hair, oils will migrate to the interior of the wig. So, make sure you wash the wig both inside and out.

Human hair wigs should be treated as though they were your real hair. It is best to use salon-formulated shampoos and conditioners because of their superior quality and their gentleness on hair. If your hairpiece is colored or permed, you will want to use products for colored and permed hair. A human-hair wig should be washed in warm water, not hot.

A synthetic-hair wig should be washed in cool water only and allowed to dry naturally. After drying, the wig will return to its original style with a few gentle shakes. Hot water, hair dryers, and curling irons should *never* be used on a synthetic wig. The plastic hairlike fibers will melt with heat.

How to wash your wig

Step 1: Turn it inside out. Scrub using shampoo with your hands and break up any oils. Thoroughly rinse it inside out.

Step 2: Now flip it right side out so the hair is on the outside. Completely drench the hair with a sprayer or shower. Do not apply shampoo or conditioner directly to the knots. This may cause the knots to slip, causing hair loss. Make sure the hair is going in a down direction so the hair does not get tangled. Whether you are shampooing the wig in the shower or sink, by keeping it in a downward position, all the dirt goes down the drain. Thoroughly rinse and blot it dry until damp. Repeat if extra dirty.

Step 3: Apply conditioner. Thoroughly rinse out the conditioner.

Step 4: Gently blot dry with a towel. Use a wide-toothed comb, not a fine-toothed one. I don't encourage blow-drying the wig, or at least not on a regular basis. Ideally, let the wig dry naturally. Blow-drying can open up the hair's cuticles and give it a rougher look, not a smooth, silky look. When the cuticles are tight and intact, when you go into the sun, the better-quality hair refracts the light. That means the sun will hit the wig, and if it's healthy, it will refract right back at you. As opposed to someone who has abused their wig, their overprocessed hair won't refract the light, and it will have a dull finish. Of course, you want your hair to look as beautiful and natural as possible. If you are in a rush and need to blow-dry, set the dryer to cool or low.

Instead of blow-drying, let it air-dry on your wig head. If you want a curl in there, scrunch the hair with your fingers while it's still damp. How long it takes to dry depends on the climate you are in. In Arizona, where I live, it's a dry heat, so it'll dry sooner. If you are living in the South, where it is hot and muggy, it may take longer to dry.

Step 5: When you take your wig off of your wig head, it will most likely require a bit of styling. That might involve wetting parts of the wig and directing it in the direction you want it to go. You may use a hot iron or flat iron on your wig if it is of good quality, but never on synthetic hair as it is made of plastic, which melts when it comes in contact with heat! Use your device on a medium setting, never on high. Perhaps you just need to use the hot iron on your bangs. Hair won't move without heat, so you might need to nudge it a bit to get it where you want it to go. Use a spray or leave-in heat protectant.

Just like your own growing hair, most wigs have a multidirectional part. Wig hair can swivel to the right or the left and part on the right or left. In the old days, you couldn't do that.

Hair care products

Taking good care of your wig includes selecting the right shampoo and conditioner for your specific type of wig. Using products designed for regular hair will harm the wig's synthetic fibers or strip natural oils from human-hair wigs. It is advisable to use a mild shampoo with low sulfate levels and conditioners that restore moisture without leaving any residue on the wig. Also, thoroughly rinse the wig to ensure no residue is left behind. With proper care, your wig will maintain its natural shine, luster, and style for months, if not years. At Peggy Knight Wigs, we have a bundle care kit we've put together that is a perfect gift for someone experiencing hair loss. It includes Peggy Knight Wigs shampoo, conditioner, masks for the ends of hair, a brush, and a wig holder. It also includes a turban like the one I use to sleep in. **[add QR code]**

Wig care

Think about your wig as fine lingerie. You would never throw your fine lingerie in the washer. You would hand-wash it. Note that if you sleep in your wig, it will wear out faster and develop tangly split ends. If you want to sleep in your hair, I advise you to buy a cheap synthetic wig that you wear only for sleeping. When it gets ruined, simply throw it away and buy another one. If you are paying good money for a human-hair wig, the last thing you want to do is sleep in it!

Wearing hats can also complicate matters. When it comes to swimming in any type of water, whether it's a lake, ocean, or chlorine pool, I recommend not wearing your wig as it will cause unnecessary wear and tear. It could possibly cause the cuticles of the hair on your wig to open up, resulting in tangling. If you are swimming laps, I highly recommend you wear a Speedo-type swim cap or buy an inexpensive wig for swimming.

Protect your hair from the sun

You should always protect your hair from the sun. Hair oxidizes in the sun. That means if you are a brunette at the beginning of the summer and play golf all week long without a hat, you will become a red blonde. Human hair is often colored prior to being made into a wig. Rarely is it "virgin" hair. I suggest wearing a hat; however, wearing hats can cause the wig to shift, and your hair might tangle, especially if it is made of low-quality hair.

I've mentioned this before, but never color your wig yourself. This is not the time to go to the grocery store and purchase your favorite boxed hair color. You need a trained wig salon stylist. This might shock you. Many factories that produce less-expensive wigs, use dyes meant for the textile trade. These dyes are intended for *carpets*!!! You can't color those kind of wigs. Your stylist will do a test color in an inconspicuous place on your wig to test. That's a good idea because I've seen colors turn the wig green!

When you go to your stylist, remember that these three words mean the same thing:

1. Lifting of color
2. Bleaching
3. Highlighting

And these three words mean the same thing:

1. Dye
2. Deposit
3. Lowlight

How to style your wig

Can I color and style my wig?

Human hair wigs can be styled on a daily basis, much like your real hair. Of course, you need to be careful when using curling irons and the like, which can damage wig hair. Human hair wigs can also be highlighted, colored, or permed by a professional stylist. Note that the processes for coloring and perming a wig requires special training and SHOULD NOT BE ATTEMPTED AT HOME. Don't forget that a human hair wig will tend to hold its color (or a perm) for quite some time since the hair does not grow out. Of course, the color will eventually oxidize or fade, and a perm will eventually relax, so these treatments will need to be repeated periodically.

Synthetic wigs cannot be highlighted or colored and cannot be restyled.

How to put on and wear a wig

Think of putting on a wig like putting on a hat. If you have hair growth, you need to tuck the hair under the cap. A good tip is to tie your remaining hair in a low ponytail first. Start by putting the front of the wig on your forehead and pulling it back over your head. Look in the mirror as you adjust the wig until the front hairline is comfortable and natural-looking. Make sure the wig is not resting on the top of the ears. You can use bobby pins to secure the wig in place or use the adjustable straps found in most wigs to adjust the size of the wig to fit your head snugly.

Wearing a wig can sometimes be tricky. First, you need to make sure it is sized correctly. If it is too loose or moving around the elastic at the nape of the neck, it should be tightened by using Velcro or hooks and eyes.

How to remove and store a wig

Removing a wig is easy. Carefully lift up the wig from each side of your temples and try to avoid messing up the style. To store the wig, place it on a mannequin head or plastic wig head and avoid exposing it to heat or direct sunlight.

How to travel with a wig

If you travel, you don't want your wig to lose its shape or get damaged in transit. You'll want to keep your wig in great condition no matter where you're headed. When traveling with your wig, you need to ensure it remains protected.

If you travel with two or more wigs, I suggest a plastic foldable wig head. The collapsible plastic travel wig stand is very lightweight and takes up almost no space in your suitcase. Alternatively, you can also use a folded towel in the shape of a mannequin head to place your wig on.

What to do if your wig gets wet

No matter what type of hair your wig is made of, water is not your enemy. The only problem is that it messes up your hairstyle. If your wig gets wet unexpectedly, you can blot it with a towel to remove excess water and let it dry naturally.

Should I expect my wig to need repair?

Almost all wigs require periodic repairs to keep them looking fresh and natural. Some repairs take just a day or a week, but others can take up to three months.

As with any head of hair, a human hair wig will lose hair due to normal combing and brushing. Hair loss occurs first along the part and at the crown. On many wigs, hair can be added back in these and other areas to maintain a natural appearance.

Tangling is caused by opened hair cuticles, but proper care can prevent this. Each human hair shaft has five to 10 cuticle layers, which are arranged like shingle layers on a house. Under normal circumstances, these cuticles lay flat, and hair is easily brushed. When human hair is permed or colored, the cuticles are opened and then closed again to complete the process.

Hand-tied synthetic wigs may need to be steamed to eliminate frizz or to be restyled. This steaming technique is difficult, requires highly controlled temperatures, and should only be done by a trained styling professional. Do not attempt to do this yourself.

How many wigs do I need?

I recommend two. No matter which type of wig you choose, it is good to have a backup. Wigs need regular care and sometimes require repair, so a backup is handy. I'm sure you are familiar with the philosophy that accidents happen. Well, they do, especially with wigs. No matter how careful you are, sometimes things happen beyond your control. For instance, a friend of mine had a swimming pool in her backyard with a high fence around it. Before swimming, she would take her wig off as she did not want to damage it. While she was swimming, a bird came, swooped her wig up, and placed it high on a tree limb to make a nest. I told her she truly created the original bird's nest hairstyle!

Another client went on a long walk with her husband. Upon returning home, she was perspiring, so she took her wig and put it on a patio table. A squirrel ran off with her wig, never to be found again.

And finally, one of my clients was in Italy visiting with family on vacation. While staying in a quaint hotel, she noticed this beautiful petite lamp on the nightstand that was the perfect size for a wig head. She gently placed her wig on the lamp and went to bed. She left the hotel room the next day for a short period of time, wearing a scarf instead of her wig. Assuming the wig would be safe on the lamp, she left it there. While she was gone, the maid came in. She turned on the light switch, which activated the light bulb in the lamp. Guess what happened? The heat from the light bulb melted her wig! She called me in a panic, desperately seeking another hairpiece. She received a new wig within two days.

These stories illustrate why having at least two wigs is a good idea. Accidents truly do happen!

What should I expect to pay for a wig, and what will my insurance cover?

Products differ dramatically in price—from less than $500 to over $7,000— depending on the materials used and the process by which they have been made. Insurance may cover all or a portion of this cost if the wig is a medical hair prosthesis that has been prescribed by a doctor. Nonprofit organizations that help people with medical hair loss often have information on how best to approach your insurer for reimbursement. Some of these organizations also have funds to help people in need purchase medical hair prostheses. As the founder of Locks of Love, I made sure our recipients received wigs free of charge.

How do I locate a reputable wig provider?

I always say, "I am the last person you want to know. However, if you are experiencing hair loss, I am the first person you want to know." Because I've been in the business for so long and have alopecia, I know what it takes to be a reputable wig provider. I am always available to answer people's questions. Here are some tips on what to do.

First, check with nonprofit organizations and support groups that work with people who suffer from medical hair loss to see if they have a list of recommended wig providers. Your dermatologist and your hairstylist may also know of reputable providers. Once you have a specific provider in mind, consult the Better Business Bureau to see whether any complaints have been filed against them.

It's a good idea to ask the wig provider the following questions before purchasing your wig:

1. Do you specialize in wigs?
2. Where did you receive your education?
3. How long have you been working with wigs?
4. What percentage of your clients wear wigs?
5. Do you provide synthetic hair, human hair, or both?
6. What is your return policy?
7. Tell me about your customer service and after-care process.
8. Do you style your wigs?
9. What about repairs?

A word of caution:

Most hairstylists were hit hard by the Covid-19 pandemic, and some turned to selling wigs as a kind of "side job" without getting any training. As a result, they sell wigs from more of a fashion perspective than than from the full perspective of your needs considering the multitude of factors I've outlined in this book. They might say things like, "Look how beautiful this wig is. It will look amazing on you!" But the truth is you want your wig to look natural. And you want the person selling you a wig to be realistic and understand your wig needs. While the idea of having long hair may be appealing to many, keep in mind that the longer your hair is, the heavier it will be on your head. And long hair, if not cleaned frequently, can look straggly. Always ask your wig provider about their education and qualifications.

Most people who come to me looking for a wig have no clue what they're buying. They need to be educated, which is one of the reasons I am writing this book. I typically spend 90 minutes educating people about wigs before we start designing one for them. Just the other day, a woman was adamant about her wig being a specific yet unusual color. I explained that in order to get that color, it would take about three months to custom-order it, and even then, it might not be exactly what she wanted. She ended up leaving with NO wig, as she would not compromise on the color. Change is hard for some, but really hard for somebody looking for a wig. I've found that the older my clients are, the less willing they are to change their hair.

Gender transition hair replacement

The topic of transgender identity has become increasingly visible in the mainstream media and society in recent years. Transgender people often experience a deep and persistent sense of gender dysphoria or discomfort with the gender they were assigned at birth. This can lead them to explore and ultimately embrace a new gender identity that is more aligned with their true sense of self. I want to stress that I'm by no means an expert on transgender identity; however, I am an expert on wigs.

Today, men who are transitioning to becoming female can change anything about their bodies. That includes changing their genitals, augmenting their breasts, and changing their facial appearance through surgery. But there's something they cannot change, which is their susceptibility to male pattern baldness. Did you know that one in every two men over age 40 experience male pattern baldness?

Male pattern baldness is characterized by a gradual loss of hair from the scalp, typically starting at the temples and crown and progressing over time. While hair loss is a natural part of the aging process, male pattern baldness occurs as a result of a combination of genetic and hormonal factors, and there's no cure for it. So, that's why it's essential to educate the transgender population about wigs.

One of my clients has been transitioning since they were a teenager. Her mother was her mentor and taught her how to buy and wear a wig. So, she wore the wig her mother selected but wasn't comfortable with it. I asked her, "Do you really want to look like your mother?" So, we met, and she literally danced out of the room. Another client was transitioning from a male to a female. At work as an IT specialist, he presented his male side. But, after leaving work, he was more feminine. As his mother was dying, he knew he wanted to go back home to her funeral and present as a *her*. She worked with me and was able to attend the funeral confidently with a great head of hair that was styled to perfection.

For someone who is transgender, choosing a wig can be an exciting yet daunting process. For many, hair is a significant aspect of their gender identity, and a wig can help them feel more like themselves.

However, the sheer number of options available can be overwhelming. There are so many questions, including:

- Do you want a natural-looking wig or one that's colorful and expressive?

- Do you want synthetic or human hair?
- How much do you want to spend?
- How do you choose the right style for your face shape and personality?

Once you've determined your budget and preferences and if you will wear your wig occasionally or full-time, it's time to start exploring your options. We offer consultations as trained professionals who can help you find the right style and fit. You want your wig to make you feel comfortable and confident in your identity.

People with trichotillomania

Another group of people who are seeking wigs are people with trichotillomania, also known as hair-pulling disorder. This is a psychological condition characterized by a strong urge to pull out hair from various parts of the body, primarily the scalp, eyebrows, and eyelashes. This compulsive behavior can lead to noticeable hair loss and cause significant distress and impairment in daily functioning. When I meet with my clients, my role is not to be their therapist. I am there as a support system. I listen to their concerns about hair loss and try to find the best option for them as we talk through it. Often, they are just looking for someone to listen to their story, acknowledge them, and let them know they are okay.

CHAPTER 4

WIGGING OUT! EVERYTHING YOU NEED TO KNOW ABOUT WIGS

Acceptance of my condition didn't mean acceptance of the status quo when it came to hair loss. When I finally found the answer to my own hair loss challenge, I knew I needed to start a business to help the thousands of people out there who were suffering just like me.

As a flight attendant, my fellow stewardesses — as they were called at the time – were always asking me questions about my hair. Keep in mind that I did a lot of intercontinental flights. I became a master at changing the subject or giving false information. I didn't want anyone to know I had alopecia, and I certainly didn't want to draw attention to myself. Shortly after my hair loss began, the **National Alopecia Areata Foundation** was formed, of which I was a founding member. I was not the only scared, lost, bald girl on the planet. Within weeks of the Foundation's formation, I met hundreds of people like me.

How my pixie saved my career

When I chose my career in the airline industry, it was a different era. When I was hired, you needed to be single, have no children, and be female. There were also weight restrictions too. Those were the rules. We had to be weighed once a month. If you didn't make the cut, you were sent home without pay. And we were required to wear girdles. It didn't matter what size or shape you were. They could tell if we were wearing one by how we looked when we walked. If we jiggled, we were sent home once again without pay. For the airlines, projecting the correct image was of the utmost importance.

Even before I wore a wig, I still had to maintain the correct appearance with my thinning hair. I wasn't excited about getting a wig back then because all the synthetic wigs in the 60s and 70s looked unrealistic. And in the airline industry, everyone needed to look alike. Our hair had to look similar, as did our makeup. I needed to look like the flight attendant standing right next to me.

I almost didn't make it into the airline industry. However, having a pixie cut saved my career. Pixie cuts were popular at the time because Audrey Hepburn had a pixie cut in a popular movie, and then, later, British supermodel Twiggy had one too. In 1968, we were required to go through six weeks of training in etiquette and grooming. We learned all kinds of things, including how to walk, how to apply makeup (we all had to wear blue eyeshadow and red lipstick, wear white lingerie, gloves, and little hats. At this time, I had big bald patches on my head to cover, so I would tease and spray my hair in order to simulate a pixie cut. Near the last day of training, we all had to get haircuts. As we lined up, I was nervous. By the time it was my turn for a haircut, the hairstylist took one look at me and said my hair was too short to cut. I truly believe that if it wasn't for my pixie haircut, they would have discovered my hair loss and not allowed me to graduate from the training program. I was so relieved.

While a flight attendant, I met and dated a well-known celebrity. Instead of calling me Peggy, he referred to me as Pixie because of my pixie hairstyle. That was when I was in my early 20s.

Years later, in my 50s, I was in San Francisco, and a friend and I went to see him perform at a casino showroom. We purchased two tickets. When we arrived, I sent a note backstage saying, "Hi Frank, it's Pixie. I haven't seen you for 40 years." I got a note back from him welcoming me and my friend backstage after the show. When our eyes met, he said, "Pixie, the years have been kind to you." I believe the reason the years had been kind to me was my youthful hair. With wigs, you can have the youthful hair you've always wanted, and that will help keep you looking young.

Becoming one with your wig

It quickly became apparent to me that the aesthetic aspect of hair loss was as important as the medical side. I took off in the direction of "finding a better mousetrap" – or, in this case, a better wig. My research took me to Australia, where I was fitted for a vacuum-type wig. I introduced this technology to the American market in 1982. It was hot and heavy, but it did not come off the head. And believe it or not, it was made with a plaster cast, and the base was fiberglass. It was the best technology at the time because it didn't come off my head. Looking back, it was such dated technology.

Here's the thing, though, when you're walking around with fiberglass on your head, it gets hot. I absolutely loved dancing. So, I'd go into the bathroom, and I take this fiberglass wig off, and I'd have a puddle of perspiration on my head, which I'd dump into the sink, and then I'd put my wig back on again and continue dancing. Looking back, I still thought it was the best technology at the time because it was the only thing that didn't come off my head. Well, we have progressed since those days. And now they use a silicone that around the perimeter of the head. I still have an original vacuum wig with a fiberglass base displayed in my hairpiece museum.

As I grew my sales network, my customer base expanded. After 28 years of selling this vacuum-type wig, a new, lighter, and more comfortable base came on the market. I now deal exclusively with a grip-type base that is as secure and much cooler than the vacuum base. While walking outside one day, I actually felt a drop of rain on my head. Technology had progressed – but the wig manufacturers took their time adopting it. In Italy, they were still making them the way their ancestors did. Eventually, they caught up to new user-friendly ways of manufacturing. The hair shedding was corrected, the quality of hair improved, and the bases and fits were customized to fit most heads. I now offer grip-type wigs and hair pieces to my clients. They stay put and look so natural; in many cases, they look even more natural than the wearer's own hair. It is a win-win for everyone. One of my cancer clients still wears a wig even after the regrowth of her own hair.

Everything you need to know about wigs

I was desperate to find a wig that would conceal the fact that I was losing – and then had lost – my hair. I would have to fashion my own to finally obtain a natural look.

First, I need to get this off my chest. I can't tell you how often people come to me and refer to wigs as units. Units? And I know why this happens. If you were a man purchasing a toupee, it would be referred to as a unit. Why? In my opinion, men can't become one with their hair. How often have you heard the term crowning glory when it comes to a woman's hair? There's a stark difference between men and women, and it shows why hair is such a psychological conundrum.

Just one more rant – never, I say *never,* call the person who sold you the wig and ask them for an install. Install? We aren't installing carpeting or putting in an air conditioner, it's a wig! When I sell a wig, I'm there to make them look beautiful, not to install it. Whoever sold you the wig should do the same.

In today's world, people with medical hair loss can now choose between many different hair replacement products. Good wigs and hairpieces will look natural and suit your needs and your life-style. The following is an introduction to the terminology that is often used to describe wigs and hairpieces.

Base Types

Net-base wigs

Net-base wigs offer flexibility. These types of wigs can generally be fitted to and worn by someone with either partial or total hair loss. Because they breathe, they are also comfortable and easy to wear. However, their fit will be less secure than that of a grip-type wig, and they may also require more care. Grip-type wigs are best for people with no hair at all. The best net-base wigs use an ultrafine net, sometimes called a "micronet," which keeps the hairs closer together, providing a more natural appearance. Some net-base designs also have a polyurethane or even a silk liner that increases comfort, ensures a more secure fit, and helps to provide a more natural-looking scalp at the part.

Net-base wigs may be ready-made or custom-made.

Silicone grip

I had been trying to cover up hair loss for 15 years when I discovered that I didn't have to put up with hiding under wraps or bad wigs that threatened to expose my bald head at any moment. At the age of 30, I found out about a revolutionary hair replacement solution – at that point available only in Australia – that used a silicone grip instead of tape or elastic to secure hairpieces to one's head. It actually worked. Security was my new friend.

For years, I had been creating my own wigs that actually looked natural. Now, finally, I had a foolproof way to keep them on my head. That's when I realized that I'd found my calling. I had to share this answer to hair loss with the millions of girls, teens, and women who still suffered the way I had. I could improve their lives just as instantly and profoundly as I had improved my own. And, with a natural head of hair that didn't constantly threaten to pop off or make their heads ache, they could once again feel as normal as I now did.

NOTE: Polyurethane does not grip the scalp. Don't be confused with silicones and polyurethane silicone bases. Silicone grips to a clean oil-free scalp. Polyurethane does not stick. You must use tape.

Design and Construction

Ready-made wigs

Ready-made wigs, which usually have a net base, are designed to fit a wide range of head sizes. The back of the wig generally has a series of eye hooks and a thin elastic band or Velcro strips that can be adjusted to make the wig fit snugly.

Ready-made wigs can be either machine-made or hand-tied. Customarily, ready-made wigs that are machine-made use synthetic hair. These wigs are lower in price and can be immediately purchased, but they rarely offer the style, comfort, and security that most people seek, and they cannot be restyled.

Ready-made wigs that are hand-tied can be made with either synthetic or human hair. Human hair provides a more natural-looking scalp and can be styled and restyled.

Semi-custom wigs

Some manufacturers offer semi-custom net-base wigs. These wigs come in a series of cap sizes and shapes, so an individual can select the cap that best approximates the shape of his or her head. Hair is usually then hand-tied onto this base to provide a natural-looking wig. It usually takes three to six months to make a semi-custom wig. It is more expensive than a ready-made wig.

Custom-made wigs

Custom-made wigs are carefully crafted to fit the precise shape of the head of an individual. Custom-made net-base wigs can be fitted and worn by someone with either partial or total hair loss, while custom-made grip wigs are designed specifically for people with total hair loss. It may take three to six months to create a custom-made wig. This wig is more expensive than a ready-made wig or semi-custom wig.

Net hairpieces are secured with an elastic band at the nape of the head. These can be tightened or loosened as needed. Some pieces have clips for a secure attachment. Double-sided tape or glue is also used to secure the wig. I do not recommend glue, as I've seen so many women get dermatitis on their scalp because of the glue. Wig grips can also be used, which are like a head-band.

The process of crafting a Velcro custom-made net-base wig begins with the creation of a scalp mold for an individual. After the natural hairline, crown, and part are traced on this mold, it serves as the model for the net base. Hair is then carefully selected to match an individual's natural or desired hair color, length, and style, and it is tied to this net base.

Handmade wigs

Most custom-made wigs utilize hand construction methods. Hair is either hand-tied on a net base or implanted by hand on a custom-molded base. Hand construction methods are considered to be superior to machine construction because the hair in a wig can be tailored to an individual client's wishes, and it will often have a more natural-looking appearance.

A word about the hairline...

One of the most critical areas in wig design is the front hairline. Many wigs do not have natural-looking front hairlines, so clients are forced to wear bangs or pull their hair forward. Most wigs these days come with a lace front design that is very natural and replicates the front hairline.

Hair Types

Synthetic hair wigs

Synthetic hair wigs are relatively inexpensive, readily available in a wide variety of colors and styles, and easily maintained.

Due to technological advancements, synthetic fibers in wig manufacturing have improved dramatically in appearance and quality, but despite these improvements, they are still stiffer than human hair and thus do not yet blow and flow in quite the same manner.

Many synthetic wig products are made with plastic fiber, which holds its color and shape. This is both a plus and a minus. Synthetic wigs will retain most of their color even with prolonged sun exposure, but they cannot be dyed or highlighted, they cannot be permed, and most cannot be restyled. They can be itchy and hot. They are not heat-resistant, and they have a shorter life span, typically two months to a year. Some hand-tied synthetic wigs can be restyled by a professional with the use of measured heat. Do not try it yourself!

I wore synthetic wigs when I was a flight attendant. I have memories of flying on intercontinental flights in one of the first Boeing 747 airplanes. It truly was a revolution in aviation technology. The 747 was taller than a six-story building and wider than a boulevard. Our galley kitchen was below the passenger deck. Remember when they used to serve meals on airplanes? If I got stuck in the galley cooking food, it could be disastrous since my synthetic wig was made of plastic. When it gets hot, it can melt, especially when opening up a hot oven. When you worked the galley, you were typically alone. One time when I got stuck working the galley, I was adamant I wasn't going to singe any more wigs as it was becoming expensive to replace them. Once en route to New York, I ruined a wig because of the hot oven. From then on, I always traveled with two wigs.

On one flight, instead of risking damaging my wig, I tied a first-class cloth napkin to my head to protect my wig. I was startled when one of the flight attendants came down and asked me why I was wearing this napkin on my head. I told them, "You would never understand." When getting off the tarmac in windy cities like Chicago, I always worried about seeing my wig rolling down the tarmac. Luckily, it never happened! However, this was one of the reasons I got into the wig business during my flying days. I was a flight attendant for 25 years until I got into the wig business full-time.

When I was a flight attendant based in Hawaii, I had big bald spots on my scalp. I was resisting getting a wig because I felt it would make me look like a fake. If I broke down and bought a wig, it would mean I accepted the fact that I was bald. It would take me hours to get ready for work. I would spend countless hours in front of the mirror looking at the back of my head. I would attempt to camouflage big bald spots on the back of my head to no avail. The trade winds are natural in Hawaii, and before I even got to work, they were destroying my hair. I never won the battle with my hair loss and wore a wig because I had to. Eventually, the trade winds won. I packed up and left the islands. There is so much psychology behind hair loss. It's good to recognize that as you forge ahead.

Human hair wigs

Human hair wigs are often more expensive than synthetic wigs, but they generally last longer, and they look and feel more natural. They can also be colored and permed (by a professional), though they will gradually lose color with sun exposure.

The hair for human hair wigs comes from many different sources. It can be derived from donations and from people who sell their hair. The hair is then sorted by color, length, texture, and curl patterns. It is then sewn onto a wig base either by hand or with a machine. About 15 years ago, I took a course in Germany on how to make wigs and tie the knots with a latch hook. It's the same type of tool used for making a rug. During the process, you had to pick up one hair and sew it into the cap. Since I knew how to crochet, I thought, I can do this! I found out I was not good at this at all. It requires an artistic person, small hands, good eyes, and experience in the industry. Some companies will knot one hair at a time. While it takes longer, it creates a higher-quality wig. To make one wig, it can take one to two weeks, depending on the skill of the person doing the knotting.

There are approximately 50 different types of knots used in hand-sewing a wig base. For example, with a man's toupee, you don't want fullness; you want it to appear flat, so that requires a particular type of knot. For people looking for bigger, fuller hair, there's a totally different type of knot used. For some cheaper human hair wigs, to cut corners, they do something called wafting, which is a string of hairs all sewn together like a hula skirt on the back of the head. It's not as natural looking as hand-sewn.

Human hair comes in many grades, the finest of which is non-processed European-quality hair. Processed hair may be stripped of its outer cuticle layers and dyed, thereby lowering its quality, shortening its life, and making it more difficult to care for.

Hand-tied wigs

Hand-tied wigs are wigs that are made with each individual hair strand being sewn into the wig cap by hand. This results in a very natural-looking hairline and density.

Machine-made wigs

Machine-made wigs are wigs that are made using a sewing machine. Strips of hair called wefts are sewn in a circular manner around the sides and back of the cap.

Half wigs - Enhancement Hair™

A half wig is a type of wig that only covers the top half of the head. They are typically used to add volume or length to the wearer's natural hair but can also be used to cover up thinning hair or bald spots. Half wigs can be attached with clips, combs, or adhesive and are available in a variety of colors and styles.

Full wigs

Full wigs cover the entire head. They can be made from real hair or synthetic fibers and are available in a variety of colors and styles. Full wigs are often used for total or partial hair loss.

A word about different types of hair. The hair of different ethnicities varies by thickness. People of Japanese and Indian descent have the thickest hair. The Chinese have the next thickest hair texture followed by Indonesians texture and Europeans, who have the finest hair texture.

Here are some facts about our hair:

- The average person has approximately 90,000 to 150,000 scalp hairs. Natural blondes tend to have the most hairs (averaging 140,000), while brunettes and redheads fall on the lower end of the normal scale (averaging 105,000 and 90,000 hairs, respectively).

- All scalp hair continually cycles through a lengthy growth period followed by a short resting phase and then loss. During the growth period, which lasts two to six years, hair emerges from a follicle and lengthens by roughly half an inch a month. It then enters a resting phase, which lasts just two to three months. After the hair is lost, new hair emerges from the same follicle within six months.

- It is normal to lose 50 to 150 hairs per day. True hair loss, or alopecia, occurs when an excessive number of hairs are lost over a short period of time or when hairs are not replaced in a timely or fully healthy fashion.

- Advanced technology, manufacturing, and design techniques have facilitated a transformation in the wig industry, with an extensive range of styles, materials, and designs available. Ultimately, the choice of the right wig depends on your individual preferences, needs, and budget. However, with advancements in the wig industry, you now have numerous options to choose from to feel confident in your appearance. Now that you know a little about all the different types of wigs available to you, you'll want to start deciding which wig is right for you.

Be cautious

Most wig sellers do not know their product line as they have not invested the time necessary to study it thoroughly. Ask lots of questions prior to purchasing your wig. Remember, knowledge is power!

CHAPTER 5

AGING HAIR IS A THING

Yes, aging hair is a thing. Hair loss is a common problem that affects both men and women. While it is often thought of as a male issue, hair loss in women is more common than many people think. In fact, studies suggest that up to 50 percent of women will experience some degree of hair loss (androgenetic loss) in their lifetime.[1]

The causes of hair loss in women can vary and may include genetics, hormonal changes, stress, illness, and certain medications. It can also be a side effect of treatments like chemotherapy or radiation therapy.

While many women experience mild or temporary hair loss, others may experience a more severe or permanent loss that can have a significant impact on their quality of life. Women may feel self-conscious or embarrassed about their hair loss and may struggle with their identity and self-esteem as a result.

Fortunately, you can have that youthful hair that you are yearning for with something called Enhancement Hair™. With Enhancement Hair™, you can regain your confidence and enjoy a fuller, more vibrant head of hair. Throughout the years, I have become an Enhancement Hair™ expert, and I'm happy to say it has been life-changing for women dealing with devastating thinning hair loss.

What does Enhancement Hair™ mean?

Enhancement Hair™ is a popular half wig for those looking to add length, volume, and fullness to their natural hair. Gone are the days when it was only celebrities who could afford to have gorgeous, flowing locks. Nowadays, Enhancement Hair™ is available to everyone, making it possible to achieve the hair of your dreams with a variety of techniques and options. When people refer to Enhancement Hair™, people often think about hair extensions. These are two different things.

Hair extensions add length or volume to your natural hair. The extensions can be made of synthetic or natural human hair. Human hair extensions are popular because they look more natural and can be styled, cut, and dyed, just like natural hair. Hair extensions are available in different styles, lengths, and colors to match your natural hair. However, I caution against hair extensions, especially for women with thinning hair.

When you have fragile hair, and you take another hunk of hair and attach it to the fragile hair, it causes loss of the remaining hair. This is referred to as traction alopecia, which is hair loss caused by repeated pulling on the hair through styling or hair care.

When you wear hair extensions, they are never placed on top of the head because they will be seen. Extensions are placed on the sides and in the back and pull on the remaining hair. If you're going to use hair extensions for a short period of time and you've got plenty of hair on the top of your head, just know that you may have hair loss due to the extensions. They are not for someone who is experiencing the female version of male androgenetic alopecia (MAA, male pattern baldness). So, if that's your situation, hair extensions are not going to help as they may cause more damage to your remaining hair. Many of my clients have used hair extensions for an extended period of time. As a result, their hair is thinning, and they don't have enough remaining hair to which to attach those extensions. So, they are now seeking Enhancement Hair™ or a full wig as a result.

Don't forget maintenance

There is more maintenance involved with Enhancement Hair™. Just like you do your nails every two or three weeks and get your hair colored every six weeks, you need to schedule regular maintenance with your Enhancement Hair™. The color of your own growing hair and the Enhancement Hair™ must always match. Both will oxidize over time, and they will do so unevenly. That's why color matching is critical for a more natural look.

Thinning hair prevalence

Women are more likely to experience diffuse hair loss, which is a gradual thinning of hair all over the scalp, rather than the patterned baldness that men experience. While men typically have a receding hairline or a bald spot on top of their head, women usually notice wider part lines or a smaller ponytail circumference.

In women, hair thinning can occur due to hormonal changes during pregnancy, menopause, and thyroid disorders. Hair loss during pregnancy is temporary and usually resolves on its own after childbirth. However, a more prolonged hair loss condition called postpartum hair loss can occur after giving birth. Women going through menopause may notice changes in their hair texture and thickness due to the decrease in estrogen. Similarly, an overactive or underactive thyroid gland can disrupt the hair growth cycle and lead to hair thinning.

On the other hand, genetics play a more significant role in male pattern baldness, but women can also inherit the genes for hair thinning. Female pattern hair loss, also known as androgenetic alopecia, can be inherited from either side of the family. This type of hair loss is characterized by a gradual thinning of the hair on the crown and the top of the scalp. It usually starts in the late 20s and early 30s.

Stress can also contribute to hair thinning, as excessive stress can trigger a condition called telogen effluvium. This is a type of hair loss that results from a disruption in the normal hair growth cycle. Stress can also lead to unhealthy hair habits, such as pulling, twisting, or rubbing the hair, which can cause breakage and damage.

Diet and nutrition are also essential factors that can affect hair health. A diet lacking in essential nutrients such as protein, iron, and vitamins can contribute to hair loss and thinning. On the other hand, a well-balanced diet rich in nutrients can promote healthy hair growth and prevent hair thinning.

Certain medications, medical conditions, chemotherapy, and radiation therapy used to treat cancer can also cause hair loss in women.

So many women don't realize that Enhancement Hair™ is an option for them. Some women are absolutely devastated by thinning or aging hair. As I consult with them, I think to myself that it looks like they have a full head of hair. However, if they have half the amount of hair they are used to, they are devastated. Women of a certain age may think of their hair as their crowning glory. I hear this all the time, "I'm known for my hair; I've always had this beautiful, thick, gorgeous hair, and now it's thin, and you can see through it, and I don't feel attractive anymore." I assure them it doesn't have to be this way. They are relieved when I tell them that they don't need to walk around with thinning hair. It can be nicely covered. I'm referring to Enhancement Hair™, which can be used every day, not just for special occasions. But you need the right Enhancement Hair™ to make it look natural.

It's as easy as 1, 2, 3, 4...

When it comes to replacement hair, it is as easy as 1, 2, 3, 4!
You need the right:

1. Color
2. Length
3. Size
4. Type of hair

Color

Matching your natural hair color is key in selecting Enhancement Hair™. But it's not as easy as you might think for several reasons. Primarily, your hair color changes. For example, the color of brown hair changes regularly. Many women color their hair to hide gray hair. Hair color changes from week to week. Sometimes people will say to me, "Well, this isn't my fresh color. My fresh color was last week, and now it's a little bit lighter." So. your hair color is constantly changing. Then when you get an enhancement piece and put it on, the color changes at its own pace. So, your enhancement topper is oxidizing, which is a normal process. And your Enhancement Hair™ is going to get lighter over time. But not as fast as dyed gray hair because dyed gray hair is still growing. So now you've got a topper, and it always has to match the hair. Otherwise, there's this line of demarcation where you go, "Oh, what happened to my hair color?"

Be aware that because your regular hair color is always changing, it requires more maintenance than a wig, as your hair will oxidize. Maintenance on your wig is about once a year, while a topper needs maintenance every six weeks. That's because of natural hair growth.

Length

Length depends on what style you want. If a woman comes in with very short aging hair and then wants Enhancement Hair™ down to their shoulders, there's not going to be enough density for an enhancement piece. You don't want the hair to be too thick. If you add more density to the top, it's going to look too "wiggy." So, it's always best to go up to two inches, but not much longer than that because then it starts looking sparse in the back.

Size

There are different sizes and shapes of Enhancement Hair™. Hair pattern loss in women is different than in men. Men with male patterned have recessed hair. Women tend to be less recessed and more diffuse in the top and back. There are all different sizes of toppers. Sizing should be chosen according to the individual pattern of loss.

Type of hair

Enhancement Hair™ comes in synthetic hair and all qualities of human hair. Human hair is the most popular type of Enhancement Hair™. They are the most natural-looking and can be treated and styled just like natural hair. Synthetic Enhancement Hair™ is man-made and made from nylon, polyester, or acrylic fibers. They come in a variety of colors, styles, and textures. A professional stylist can suggest the best option to match your own growing hair.

That's it! Once you achieve those four steps, you can blend the Enhancement Hair™ with your growing hair with amazing results. It's really important to match your own growing hair. It can get complicated when your natural hair is gray. Typically, people go down to the drugstore and purchase a box of hair color and dye their hair. The problem is that your Enhancement Hair™ won't match the color of your newly colored hair. Chances are it's an odd color if not colored professionally.

Who buys Enhancement Hair™?

It used to be women in their 60s through 80s who purchased Enhancement Hair™ from my business. However, that has changed. Most people in their 70s and 80s simply aren't going to spend a lot of money on nice hair. So, my demographic has shifted. Women in their 30s, 40s, and 50s approach me after spending lots of money on hair growth shampoos and seeing doctors because of their hair loss. They are at a loss and don't know where to go to get help. They are suffering from depression as a result. I tell them I have a solution to their problem, and it's Enhancement Hair™. The quality of hair makes or breaks your overall look and longevity. Just like buying a wig, if you buy a cheap Enhance Hair™ piece, it's going to tangle, and it's not going to blend with your own hair.

Who can benefit from Enhancement Hair™?

It's probably best to share who *can't* benefit from a topper. It's those people who don't actually have hair growing on their heads. Because if it's not enough, then you can't attach the enhancement base to their head. The topper has little clips called French clips, and they clip to the remaining hair. And if there's not enough hair, there's no place to clip it, so, it doesn't stay on. Keep in mind that some enhancement pieces are super bulky and heavy on your head. The heavier it is, the more it pulls on your remaining hair. So, it's really important to get a very lightweight piece. You do not want anything that will damage your own hair. Once you decide

Enhancement Hair™ might be right for you, you'll want to make sure you know how to place the Enhancement Hair™.

How do I place my Enhancement Hair™ on my head so it looks natural and stays secure?

There are a couple of ways of putting it on:

1. **Clip it.** The clip has silicone backing, so it's not going to break your existing or your remaining hair. The clips are probably the most secure way to adhere Enhancement Hair™ to your head. I am anti-glue, which is not meant to go on your scalp. Because glue doesn't stick to the remaining hair effectively, you need to be constantly shaving your growing hair. And another thing, it smells because you can't wash your scalp. One of my clients told me her head itched. It's no surprise as she had dermatitis, and she didn't even know it. No wonder she itched so much! Eventually, it needs to be taken off as your hair grows. Eventually, the glue is not going to stick to the remaining hair since it is growing.

2. **Use double-sided tape.** The use of tape and clips is a good option for those with thin hair who have some hair on the sides and back. You simply cut a little off of the double-sided tape, stick it to your scalp, and then apply your enhancement hair. The tape will stick to both your scalp and the enhancement hair, keeping it firmly in position.

How do I style my Enhancement Hair™, or do I need a special hairstylist?

You need to find a hairstylist that can work with Enhancement Hair™. You need a stylist who knows how to cut and blend your natural hair with the Enhancement Hair™. It can be tricky. They aren't taught these skills in beauty school. There are special skills required to style wigs and toppers. Having a good stylist is key. I always refer my clients to a local stylist. If they want their own stylist to continue doing their hair, I send their stylist educational videos.

Does it matter where I purchase my hair?

In short, yes, it matters! Lots of companies sell inexpensive hair and wigs on the internet and offer no customer service. It's best to purchase from a company that provides excellent customer service. Beware of the "surprise in a box" scenario. The hair may look beautiful on the internet, but you receive something very different. I had that experience two weeks before my wedding. After days of crying, I found a hat instead of a veil.

Wigs, Enhancement Hair™, and activities

My clients often ask me, "Can I swim in this?" My response is always the same, "I wouldn't." If wearing a wig or hairpiece is important to you while swimming, I advise you to buy a cheap hairpiece because you don't want to ruin your hair because of the chlorine or saltwater. They're going to play havoc with your hair. I also advise wearing a baseball cap or Speedo swim cap.

I have two very nice wigs that I use for activities. I have two that I wear for swimming and for when I'm out in the sun, although you want to avoid direct sun on your hair, for example, while golfing. If you're out every day for four to five hours in direct sun and your hair is not covered, it will oxidize much faster. So, you want to prevent that from happening.

Sleeping

One of the worst things for your hair is sleeping on it. While sleeping in your wig or Enhancement Hair™, as you move your head on the pillow, you cause friction. If you're in a situation where you don't want to sleep without a wig, you can wear a cheap one that matches your hair. However, chances are, whoever you're trying to prevent from knowing you are wearing a wig or Enhancement Hair™, probably already knows you are wearing it.

Why am I so cold?

We lose much of our body heat through our heads. So, anyone without hair, whether it's due to chemo, alopecia, or aging hair loss, is going to lose more body heat than others. I can't sleep at night without my head covered because I get cold, so I wear a sleep cap made of bamboo. It's soft, absorbent, and very pretty, and it comes in a variety of colors.

Wigs are great in the winter because you're wearing an automatic cap on your head to keep you warm. But in the summer, it can get hot. Again, it depends on the quality of the piece. Better quality wigs are thinner and cooler.

Summing up

Hair loss can be a distressing experience for women, and it is important for them to have options that can help them regain their confidence and boost their self-esteem. Enhancement Hair™ has become a popular solution for women with hair loss or thinning hair. It is a non-surgical, non-invasive procedure that can increase the volume, length, and thickness of hair, providing a natural-looking finish. Additionally, Enhancement Hair™ allows women to experiment with different hairstyles and colors, giving them the freedom and flexibility to express themselves. Overall, Enhancement Hair™ is a practical and efficient option for women with hair loss, offering them a viable solution for their hair concerns.

Sources:

1. https://my.clevelandclinic.org/health/diseases/16921-hair-loss-in-women#:~:text=However%2C%20it%20is%20estimated%20that,women%20in%20the%20United%20States

CHAPTER 6

ADVICE FOR PARENTS WHEN IT COMES TO KIDS AND HAIR LOSS

Losing hair when you're a child is particularly challenging. I know firsthand how cruel kids can be. That's why Peggy Knight Wigs has developed hair replacements specifically designed for the younger set.

I remember my first wig-buying experience as a kid. Unlike today, wig shops were nonexistent, but after an extensive search, we finally found a department store that offered wigs for sale. The entire family piled into the car, and we drove to the city. Out on a table sat an array of wigs in different colors and lengths. I was immediately drawn to a long, very dark brown hairpiece. Where can I try it on? Does it fit? Is this the right color? With no privacy or mirrors available, I resorted to a broom closet and a compact mirror. (To this day, I shudder at those memories.) We bought it and hurried back home so I could style it to my liking.

Well, in my early days of wig-buying, the hair was not prepared as it is today. I was unable to wash the hair, as this would make it tangle. Vapon dry cleaning solution was the way to clean hair wigs back then, so I had the constant clinging odor of a busy dry cleaner's shop. Nevertheless, I had hair on my head, and it did not fall off. It was a blessing that hairstyle fashions were big and puffy in those early days because that is exactly what I had perched on my head: a big 60s bouffant style. Today, thankfully, fashionable hair is much more natural, and big hair is out.

Hair loss in children can be a very distressing experience for parents. Hair problems in children are more common than you might think and can be due to various factors and conditions. One of these is alopecia areata, which causes patchy hair loss in children. As the immune system attacks the hair follicles, resulting in round hair loss patches, the hair may fall out completely within a few weeks. Although the time period can vary, for me, it took 10 years.

I am often asked by a parent how young is too young for a child to wear a wig. The answers vary according to the individual child, but in general, I would say no younger than seven. Once a child starts grade school, it is time to get serious. Parents should start their wig research before then but hold off on buying anything. If they buy the wig too early, it will most likely end up in the toy box. However, if you feel it is vital for your child under seven to have a wig, purchase an inexpensive one. But don't be surprised to find that your child views it as a toy and only wears it once or twice. The bottom line is that parents will do anything to make their child whole. In fact, hair loss is often more upsetting to the parent than to the child. Most kids are oblivious to the fact that they are different from other kids until they hit the age of seven and peer pressure kicks in.

Tanya J., my longtime friend and customer, shares her story about hair loss that began when she was a child.

My story starts when I was a little girl, and I lost my hair and was forced to wear my first wig. The story I told myself was that God needed hair for another little girl who was less able to deal with her loss. Therefore, I was giving unselfishly to help another who was less fortunate. I believed that God knew what He was doing then, and this is still my belief today. I learned to give back to others at an early age, even though I did not understand it then. My first lesson was giving of myself, and the second lesson was learning to accept my loss.

I realized that it was okay to be different and learned to love myself for my differences. Acceptance of myself and others was something I learned at a very early age. It was not always easy, and there were times I did not want to go to school. Nevertheless, I was a trouper and took it in stride.

Instead of thinking of a wig as something negative, I turned it around and thought of it as my accessory for the day. Like my shoes and purse, I could change it depending on my mood. Instead of running from questions like, "Is that your real hair?" I answered, "Yes, want to see my receipt?" I guess the experience gave me thick skin, but the way I look at it, everyone has something. Mine just happened to be the loss of my hair. I soon became obsessed with my hair and makeup. It was so easy to drop off my wig for styling and come back the next week to pick it up with a fresh and attractive style. Do I need to tell you I was something of a diva back then?

My most difficult times were my dating years. I had to decide if I should tell my date right up-front or wait until he discovered it. I decided to tell up-front, then if he was okay with my bald head, we just might have a chance at continuing a relationship. It was kind of like taking someone's temperature. My first love was okay with me running around the house wigless but would never touch it. One day, I opened my eyes and saw him standing in front of me with my wig on his head. That was the day I fell deeply in love with him.

Now to tickle your funny bone. I was getting ready for work one day and could not find my hair. I looked high and low all over the *house. I didn't have backup hair at the time (although I can assure you that has since changed), and I couldn't imagine where it had gone. As I went to feed my cat, I noticed that she was looking at me nervously. Instantly, I knew what had happened. I looked in all of her usual hiding places, finding many long-forgotten cat toys, when lo and behold, I saw it: under the sofa, all wet and chewed up. I called in sick for the day and spent the afternoon washing and caring for my beautiful hair. I still love my cat, but my hair will never again be within her reach.*

This cat caper taught me a lesson about having multiple wigs. After a while, I had them in different colors. Each different head of hair had a name and a style to match. My favorite was Sandy Sultry. This color brought out my alter ego. I could be a different person daily. It was such fun getting up in the morning and deciding who to be and what to wear.

I met a woman with alopecia at one of the conferences. She told me that she always hid from her friends and neighbors. One day, she put on makeup and big, beautiful earrings, then walked out of her door with her head held high – and that was her last day of wearing a wig. I was so impressed with her confidence but am personally unable to appear in public completely bald. I guess my wig is my security blanket to the outside world.

Soon, I learned to focus on my inner self by understanding the stages of grief and loss. Alopecia is my teacher, and I go back to my thoughts as a little girl: God made me this way so I can be a mentor to others dealing with loss.

When you think you have bottomed out, look to those of us who have walked your same path. I would not be the successful, happy person I am today without the lessons learned from my loss.

Becky has been a customer for almost 20 years, and she graciously shares her story of being diagnosed with alopecia at age three.

We lived in a small town in Wisconsin at the time. Our family doctor diagnosed my condition and said my hair loss would probably come and go throughout my life. This was not a satisfactory explanation, and my family wanted answers. They blamed everything and everyone. My loss started at the nape of the neck. As a child all I dreamed about was to have a ponytail. As the spots grew in size, it was apparent that my ponytail dream would never come true. All of my friends wore their hair in a ponytail, and it was not fair. During my freshman year of high school, I had to wear a wig in order to cover the ever-growing bald spots. This was one of the hardest times of my life. How could I explain the sudden addition of hair? Well, I got over it and lived a normal life and was accepted by all of the kids.

Years later, after I was married and had children, my hair loss accelerated. I was completely bald. I tried everything known to the medical community and even experimented with treatments not known. One of these treatments caused blisters on the head. Cortisone injections directly into the scalp were painful and worked for a bit but never resulted in full regrowth. I remember one time I drove to Seattle with a shoebox filled with my fallen hair.

At long last, after many years of taking my hair loss journey alone, I found support from the National Alopecia Areata Foundation. I became an information junkie and researched everything available. I had always wanted to be a hairstylist, while friends thought I was crazy. "How could a bald woman become a hairstylist to others with natural hair?" It was my calling: I wanted to help people have great hair. I went to beauty school, got licensed, then began selling and styling wigs.

After working with so many chemo customers, my mother was diagnosed with cancer. I took time to be with my family and distanced myself from hairpieces. I now manage a chain of hair salons in the western United States. To this day, I find nothing quite as satisfying as helping women through their hair loss journey.

Inspirational quotes from Becky:

Parents *are afraid of what children and friends say and think about the loss of their mother's hair. Be your real self and an example to your children. Be proud of who you have become and say so to yourself and other family members. Own it!*

An older schoolmate had a very ugly wig. She would take it off when playing sports. I wish I had the guts to remove my hair in public and feel good about it. I am still in hiding.

Children: *Know you are not alone. Enroll in support groups. Educate classmates. Be bald and be proud! It is not contagious, and you will not die from it. Remember: God made some heads perfect and covered others with hair.*

Be bald and be proud!

Younger children are resilient and often don't know they are any different than the other kids on the playground. Some of my brave young clients teach me lessons about life without hair. They stand tall with their follicle-less heads held high and defy negative comments. They enter the world as proud individuals. I am so proud of these young people and absorb their confidence. Be bald and be proud! We have come a long way, my friends.

For those who choose to wear hair, we have wigs ranging from sizes **XXXS** to **XL**. We can fit almost any head size, which is the reason we do not worry about the hair slipping off the head (particularly important for children who play sports). As the old saying goes, size matters! This is especially true with wig sizing. Additionally, we adjust the density of hair to reflect the age of a child. Fine hair, and less of it, is best for children.

Traditional wigs have too much hair for children. It is important to order a wig with a light density or, if it's a ready-made wig, order for a child. The cap size is also important, so the wig does not fly off during playground recess time.

Parents often suffer guilt when it comes to their child's hair loss. Look into your family history and see if another family member has alopecia areata or another autoimmune condition. It may surprise you to discover that 20 percent of people will find a family connection. See the Medical Guide at the end of the book for more information.

CHAPTER 7

MEDICAL CAUSES
FOR HAIR LOSS

Flip through the pages of a fashion magazine and click through the television channels and count the number of hair care product ads showcasing stunning models with flowing, silky, shiny hair. What messages are these advertisements selling? In our culture, hair is associated with beauty, youth, and sexuality. Now, imagine watching these images flash before your eyes as you are experiencing hair loss and eventually going bald.

There are many medical causes for true hair loss, including:

- **Androgenetic alopecia, often called male or female pattern hair loss:** The most common type of hair loss for both men and women is androgenetic alopecia, more often called male or female pattern hair loss. In the United States alone, an estimated 50 million men and 30 million women are affected.

- **Alopecia areata:** Alopecia areata is a highly unpredictable autoimmune skin disease that may lead to the loss of hair on the scalp and elsewhere on the body. This disease affects males and females of all ages and races, but it often begins in childhood.

- **Burns and scars:** Hair loss on tissue that is badly burned or scarred has long been thought to be permanent, but a recent discovery in the field of cell research brings hope that new skin and hair may someday be grown from adult stem cells.

- **Cancer and cancer treatments (chemotherapy and radiation):** Cancer and cancer treatments can cause hair loss.

- **Diabetes:** People with diabetes are very susceptible to skin problems, which often lead to hair loss. Because of poor blood circulation, diabetics heal more slowly and scar more often from injuries, cuts, and scrapes.

- **Hormonal imbalances, pregnancy, and thyroid disease:** Hormonal changes and imbalances, no matter what the cause, often result in hair loss.

- **Infection:** Fungal and bacterial infections cause temporary hair loss.

- **Lupus:** Like diabetes, lupus, which is an autoimmune disease, may lead to hair loss for many different reasons.

- **Malnutrition, including iron deficiency:** Malnutrition, whether due to poor diet or eating disorders like anorexia and bulimia, often leads to hair loss.

- **Medications and medical treatments:** Many different medications and medical treatments can cause either temporary or permanent hair loss. Cancer treatments are notorious for this.

- **Stress, trichotillomania, and other illnesses:** Over 30 specific diseases, including diabetes and lupus, as well as diseases of the liver, kidney, and thyroid, are known to cause permanent or long-term hair loss.

I urge you to consult a medical doctor to determine the cause of your hair loss. I've created a hair loss guide that goes in-depth on each of these medical causes of hair loss, which can be found at the back of this book.

What you should know

Hair loss is more common than you think. An average person loses 100 strands a day. By the age of 30, 25 percent of men and 12 percent of women lose hair. Because our identities are so tied to our hair, not only is it a physical condition, there are psychological aspects too.

Hair loss (alopecia) can affect just your scalp or your entire body. It can be the result of heredity, hormonal changes, medical conditions, or a normal process of aging. An estimated 65 percent of cancer patients experience hair loss as a result of chemotherapy.[1] According to the American Cancer Society, cancer patients may lose their hair when chemotherapy drugs damage hair follicles, making hair fall out. Even when they are taking the exact same drugs, some patients will lose their hair while others will not. The drugs can cause hair thinning or hair loss in the scalp, pubic hair, arm and leg hair, eyebrows, and eyelashes.

Alopecia unexpectedly in the spotlight

Back in 2022, at The Oscars, Jada Pinkett-Smith found her struggle with hair loss in the spotlight. Her husband, Will Smith, slapped The Oscars host, Chris Rock when he joked about her shaved head while onstage. The now-infamous slap grew widespread support for Jada and her struggle with alopecia.

Jada talked about her hair loss in a 2018 episode of *Red Table Talk*. She shared that people had been asking her why she had been wearing turbans. She revealed that she had been experiencing "issues" with hair loss. One day while in the shower, handfuls of her hair came out in her hands. That's when she decided to cut her hair short and lamented how she loved having the freedom to

---

1 Trueb, R. M. "Chemotherapy-induced hair loss." *Skin Therapy Lett* 15, no. 7 (2010): 5-7.

have any hairstyle she pleased and now she had no choice but to go extremely short or bald.

Jada's vulnerability and willingness to share have brought about a change in the attitude of people with alopecia. Younger people, especially, are beginning to take pride in their hair loss. Historically, so many people had so much shame, and now young people are owning it and rocking it and walking around without wigs. Their bald heads are becoming a badge of honor. It's so nice to see. Young women are coming into their own power. This is because we as humans are evolving. I'm so happy that people with alopecia became inspired and more comfortable sharing their condition with others.

How common is thinning hair?

Hair loss is a common condition that affects millions of people worldwide, including men and women of all ages. According to the Cleveland Clinic, 30 to 40 percent of women over the age 40 will experience hair loss. One type of hair loss that is particularly common is androgenetic hair loss or male or female pattern baldness. Androgenetic hair loss is a type of hair loss that is largely determined by genetics and hormones. In this condition, hair starts thinning and falling out in specific patterns, which can be distressing and affect a person's self-esteem. For women, it can be more devastating to have thinning hair than total hair loss. With total hair loss, they can choose a wig, while with thinning hair, they need to decide whether or not to invest in Enhancement Hair™ or just attempt to style their hair in a way that disguises the hair loss.

This may sound counterintuitive, but it is harder to have thin or partial hair loss than it is to have total hair loss. With partial hair loss, the client must match colors and styles. With total loss, the process is easy. With a good style, it is ready to go out the door. There's no need to make sure the hair matches existing growth hair.

One client of mine feels so victimized by her hair loss because she believes her hair defines her. She actually cries when she looks at her photo. In fact, she's afraid to leave the house. She is married but is convinced her husband doesn't love her because she is losing her hair.

My client's case makes a key point—losing your hair takes a big hit on a woman's self-esteem. She isn't the only one defined by her hair. Most of us are in some way. Every hair on our body has a purpose, but we consider our hair adornment. Think about it: Our hair protects us from the sun and protects our eyes from dust. We identify with our locks. The reality is we are the person behind the hair; our hair doesn't define us.

What causes hair loss or thinning hair?

Hair loss or thinning hair can be troublesome for anybody, particularly for women. Losing hair can affect women's self-esteem, leading to anxiety or depression. There are many reasons behind hair loss or thinning hair, such as genetics, age, hormonal changes, nutrient deficiencies, and stress. Here are a few other common ones:

Covid-19

According to medical experts, Covid-19 did not directly cause hair loss. However, some people who have recovered from Covid-19 have reported experiencing hair thinning as they attempt to manage stress from having Covid-19 and any resulting nutritional deficiencies.

Aging

Hair loss can be a result of aging due to decreased estrogen and testosterone production. And as our follicles become less efficient at producing hair, the result may be thinner or sparser locks. Poor diet, stress levels, and genetics may also play a part in contributing to hair loss as we get older.

Chemotherapy

Hair loss is one of the most common side effects of chemotherapy, a common treatment for cancer in which powerful drugs are used to kill cancer cells in the body. This is because chemotherapy drugs are designed to target rapidly dividing cells, and hair cells are some of the fastest-dividing cells in the body.

These drugs interfere with the natural growth phase of the hair cell cycle, causing hair to fall out. Hair loss from chemotherapy can occur anywhere on the body, but it is most noticeable on the scalp, where hair loss can range from thinning to complete baldness.

If you ask a woman who has been diagnosed with breast cancer what is she more fearful of – losing a breast or losing her hair, about 99 percent of the time, she will say that her biggest fear is hair loss.

The degree of hair loss from chemotherapy varies depending on the type and dosage of drugs used, as well as the person's susceptibility to hair loss. Some people may experience more severe hair loss than others, while some may experience only slight thinning or no hair loss at all. While hair loss from chemotherapy is typically temporary, hair regrowth usually happens once the treatments are completed. However, it may take several months for the hair to grow back to its pre-treatment thickness or length, and the regrown hair may be of a different texture or color.

New treatment for alopecia areata receives FDA approval

On June 13, 2022, the U.S. Food and Drug Administration (FDA) approved Olumiant (baricitinib) for the treatment of severe alopecia areata in adults. This marks the first-ever approved treatment for the disease. Baricitinib is part of the class of drugs known as JAK inhibitors and is the first of several JAK inhibitors that have completed late-stage clinical trials for alopecia areata patients.

CHAPTER 8

AM I A CANDIDATE FOR PERMANENT MAKEUP TATTOOING?

Before I share how to determine if you are a good candidate for makeup tattooing, let me share my first experience with tattooing in the early days.

Early days of tattooing

Being no stranger to trying new things (including those painful cortisone shots in my scalp), I was one of the first to get my eyebrows tattooed. It was done by a man in Sausalito, California. He learned the tattooing trade in the Navy. Tattoos have been a longstanding part of military culture, with soldiers using them to signify important milestones, achievements, or even entire military careers. The United States Navy has a long tradition of sailors getting tattoos, especially tattoos of anchors.

My tattoo artist was an expert on tattooing anchors on sailors' arms. He was well known in the Bay Area for doing so. So, I don't know why I thought he'd be a natural at tattooing my eyebrows, but I was desperate. It turned out pretty awful. In fact, it looked like two caterpillars walking across my face! Once again, it came back to skin tone, something a tattoo artist specializing in anchors on arms wouldn't consider. Thus, with my olive complexion, my brown eyebrow tattoo came across as lavender and green. I truly was a guinea pig in this experiment as the tattoo artist had never attempted anything like this. Did I mention I was desperate? Because I have alopecia, I don't have any hair on my skin. So, waking up with eyebrows sounded like a great idea at the time.

Not only did this straight line above my eyes look odd, it was dangerous. However, cosmetic tattooing did not become widely regulated until the 1990s. This was partially due to concerns about the spread of infectious diseases such as HIV and hepatitis B. Today, licensed practitioners are required to use sterile equipment, follow proper hygiene protocols, and undergo regular training and certification.

With the advent of modern technology, cosmetic tattooing has continued to evolve and innovate. For example, some practitioners now use digital machines to create more precise and uniform strokes. Others use specialized pigments designed to match each client's skin tone and texture.

Reality check: Although the end result can be beautiful, tattooing does fade over time so make sure you use your sunscreen. And it is painful as everyone has a different tolerance to pain; what may be unbearable for one person may be bearable for another. The level of pain you feel during a tattoo also depends on the size, style, and location of the tattoo. Some parts of the body are more painful due to their proximity to bones, nerves, and thin skin. Make sure your tattoo artist uses a numbing agent on your brow area before starting the tattoo process.

For me, getting my eyebrows tattooed was painful. The first three quarters of my brow weren't as painful as the last quarter simply because of my thin skin.

What is paramedical tattooing and is it the same as makeup tattooing?

Paramedical tattooing, also known as medical tattooing or micropigmentation, is a form of semi-permanent tattooing that can help improve the appearance and functionality of scarred or damaged skin. It can be used to enhance or restore the appearance of various facial features. It is often referred to as makeup tattooing. This specialized technique involves implanting pigment into the skin to recreate the skin's natural color, texture, and contour, making it an ideal solution for those who have undergone surgical procedures, accidents, and burns as it achieves a natural-looking result.

If you don't want your tattoos to fade, you'll want someone who specializes in paramedical makeup.

The benefits of makeup tattooing include the convenience of not having to apply makeup daily, which saves time and money. It is also beneficial to those with alopecia or those who have difficulty applying makeup due to vision impairments or mobility issues. Additionally, makeup tattooing is long-lasting and can provide a more natural look than traditional makeup.

There are various types of makeup tattooing, including eyebrow tattooing, eyeliner tattooing, and lip tattooing. Eyebrow tattooing can help create a fuller, defined eyebrow shape, while eyeliner tattooing can make the eyes appear larger and more awake. Lip tattooing can help add color and definition to the lips, giving a more youthful appearance.

Don't forget that makeup tattooing is a permanent procedure, so it is essential to research and choose a reputable and skilled practitioner. Proper aftercare is also crucial to ensure the best results and minimize the risk of infection.

What to consider before getting a makeup tattoo

Getting a makeup tattoo or cosmetic tattoo is a form of permanent makeup that can enhance and define certain facial features. However, just like any other cosmetic procedure, it's important to consider various factors before deciding to get a makeup tattoo. Here are some factors to consider:

1. **Skin type:** The first factor to consider is one's skin type. People with oily skin may find that their makeup tattoo fades faster than those with dry skin. Additionally, people with sensitive skin may experience unwanted side effects like redness, itching, or inflammation.

2. **Medical conditions:** People with certain medical conditions like autoimmune disorders, diabetes, or blood disorders should discuss their medical history with a licensed cosmetic tattoo artist. Such medical conditions may increase the risk of infection, allergic reaction or prevent proper healing. So, it's essential to make sure you have a candid conversation with the artist about your medical history.

3. **Allergy testing:** Before getting a makeup tattoo, one should consider undergoing testing to determine any allergic reactions. People who react to regular makeup products will often react to cosmetic tattoos as well.

4. **Finding a skilled artist:** It's crucial to find a qualified and experienced cosmetic tattoo artist to ensure that the procedure is done correctly. A qualified artist will sterilize their equipment before use and possess valid licenses/certifications from recognized associations.

5. **Aftercare:** Aftercare is an extensive part of the makeup tattoo procedure. The artist will advise and provide a post-tattoo care regimen to ensure that the tattooed area heals correctly. It's essential to consider the aftercare process, as it will involve

avoiding sweating, sun exposure, and makeup for a few days to prevent infection and irritation.

While getting a makeup tattoo can provide many benefits, you should consider the factors mentioned above before making a decision. Consulting with an experienced artist, understanding the procedure's requirements, and doing thorough research can help you make an informed decision.

Paramedical makeup

Paramedical makeup is often used in combination with other medical treatments, such as laser therapy, skin grafts, or micro-needling, to enhance the healing process and achieve better aesthetic results. It is applied by trained professionals and requires a detailed consultation to determine the right color, texture, and application technique for the patient's needs.

Overall, paramedical makeup can be a valuable tool for patients who want to improve the appearance of their skin and boost their confidence while undergoing medical treatment or living with a chronic condition.

When tattoos are done properly, they are absolutely beautiful. They are done with a needle with multiple strokes. Often, this is referred to as bleeding of pigment, which takes those fine strokes and softens them, and blends them together.

These tattoos are used to enhance or restore a person's appearance after a medical procedure or condition. Common examples include nipple tattoos for breast cancer survivors or eyebrow tattoos for those who have lost their eyebrows due to chemotherapy.

Make sure your tattoo artist is certified. Many certified tattoo artists can do eyeliner, lips, and eyebrows and often work with plastic surgeons.

Meeting makeup royalty

I was on a television show in LA and the woman who did my makeup for the show that day was Candace Westmore. Her father was the famous Marvin Westmore, who is a six-time Emmy-nominated Hollywood makeup artist. He spent over 35 years in consumer makeup in the motion picture and television industry and did all the makeup for old motion pictures. His grandfather was Bud Westmore, who did the makeup for silent movies. I was a guest speaker at their company, Westmore Academy, where they specialized in paramedical makeup. At the time, they specialized in working with port wine stains. As Candace was applying my makeup, she used an old wooden box that was once her grandfather's. It truly was a highlight for me.

CHAPTER 9

LOOKING YOUR BEST: SUCCESSFULLY APPLYING YOUR MAKEUP

Makeup can transform somebody's appearance, boost their confidence, and accentuate their best features. If you have alopecia or are undergoing chemotherapy, makeup can be really tricky, especially when it comes to your eyebrows and eyelashes. I'll share with you secrets on how to create a natural look and be successful in your makeup application. Most people don't know how to apply makeup with a light hand. You definitely want to avoid looking like a clown!

I realize that some people don't wear makeup and that is totally their choice. Even though my mom had alopecia, she never wore eyelashes, and for eyebrows, she simply took a crayon and drew a straight line over her eyes to mimic eyebrows. She honestly didn't care how it looked, and that was okay. However, for me, applying makeup properly has helped instill more confidence in myself, especially on this long journey with alopecia. I know it's helped other women as well. That's why I'm sharing it here with you.

When learning how to apply your makeup, remember that practice makes perfect!

Cosmetic selection

Make sure you select waterproof or at least water-resistant cosmetics. When you are perspiring in everyday activity or while being active outdoors, you'll want water-resistant cosmetics. The last thing you want to do is wipe your brow and have your eyebrows erased because you sweat. I don't spend a lot of money on my cosmetics as there are a lot of good ones out there that aren't costly.

Keeping it clean

Your makeup brushes should be cleaned regularly. Then, let them thoroughly air-dry. Otherwise, they could be harboring bacteria, which is never good. Especially if you have cancer, your eyes are more susceptible to infections of the eye and cosmetics that are dirty can be dangerous. All eyebrow pencils should be sharpened regularly, and the tips wiped with alcohol.

Keeping up with the latest trends

Many women who have been wearing wigs for a while might believe that they need to have bangs, or their hair will look "wiggy." They prefer bangs because they want to cover their eyebrows. This is no longer necessary. Because the new wigs have beautiful lace fronts, they no longer look "wiggy."

Applying the perfect eyebrow

You'll want your eyebrows to look as natural as possible. And with today's makeup, you can achieve that. Eyebrow pencils of today have lower wax content, and they don't smudge. In contrast, eyeliner pencils have a higher wax content so that it allows you to smudge it and get that smoky eye look.

With an eyebrow pencil, some have an applicator that allows you to apply five strokes at once. You can also use multiple colors using very small strokes.

Applying the perfect lash

You are probably well aware of the popularity of eyelash extensions. Eyelash extensions have become a trendy beauty treatment in recent years. If you have no eyelashes or you are losing your eyelashes, obviously, you won't be getting eyelash extensions. However, there is a great way to get long, voluminous lashes and that is through false eyelashes. Applying false eyelashes can be a daunting task, especially as you start out. However, once practiced, and perfected, false eyelashes can elevate any makeup look to the next level. **[insert video]**

First, you'll want to choose the right false eyelashes. False eyelashes come in various lengths, thicknesses, and styles, so it's important to choose one that complements your eye shape and desired look.

Now it's time to measure and trim the false eyelashes to fit your eye shape. Hold the eyelash strip against your lash line to get an idea of how much you need to trim from the outer corner. Use small scissors to trim the excess, making sure to cut from the outer edge rather than the inner corner.

Getting your eyes ready

Apply powder foundation on the eyebrows and eyelids as glue tends to stick better if it is applied to powder. I apply eyeshadow that is lighter to my upper lids and darker shadow to my lower lid. Then, it's time to apply the glue. Wait until it is not completely dry, rather you want it to be tacky. Place the eyelash on the tacky glue with tweezers while looking in the mirror. You want your eyelashes to look the same for both eyes. The last thing you want is one lash going up and the other going down. After you apply, let it completely dry and finish your makeup routine.

I apply my eyeliner after I put my lashes on. I take the eyeliner and connect the dots as my eyelash is only on three-quarters of my eye. I line the top, then line the bottom. Note that I typically wear my eyelashes for a few days and then give my eyes a rest. If I keep my eyelashes on for too long, my eyes get inflamed.

How much time it takes to do your makeup depends on whether it is your first time or if you do it as part of your daily beauty routine. When I was a flight attendant, our makeup had to be impeccable, and sometimes it would take hours to get it right. One morning I was having a tough time. I was married at the time, and I came out of the bathroom with big alligator tears, throwing a hissy fit. My husband asked what was going on. My eyes were red and swollen from crying. He then exclaimed, "Oh, look at what is on your cheek!" I had no idea my lash had slipped off. I would have gone to work with an eyelash on my cheek! He did everything he could not to laugh at me!

My advice is just to keep practicing with your makeup, especially those eyelashes! Applying your eyelashes can be as tedious as doing embroidery, especially if you don't know what you are doing. Your eyelashes can slip off of your eyes if you don't allow the glue to dry. Oh, and you can get glue in your eye. After that, you can't correct the situation as your eye and eyelid are swollen. So, take it off, go about the day, and the next morning try it again. Once you get the hang of it, it's like being an excellent artist.

The glue that adheres to the eyelashes comes in black or clear. I like black because it acts like eyeliner. It works for me because I'm brunette; however, if you are blonde, you will want the transparent glue, so it looks more natural. You'll then fill in everything with eye shadow.

To ensure the false eyelashes adhere well and stay in place throughout the day, apply a thin layer of lash glue onto the band of the false lashes. It's essential to wait a few seconds for the glue to become tacky before applying the lashes. Doing so will help prevent the lashes from sliding around and make the application process smoother.

Starting from the outer corner, carefully place the false eyelashes onto your lash line. Use a pair of tweezers or your fingers to adjust the false lashes and ensure they're sitting comfortably on your lash line. Applying the false lashes slightly above your natural lash line can help create the illusion of larger, more dramatic eyes.

You'll want to make sure the glue is extra secure so one of your eyelashes won't flip up. Which reminds me that you want your eyelash glue to be fresh, meaning it isn't past its expiration date or has been open for too long. So, if you see eyelash glue on sale at your local drugstore, don't rush to buy 12 to stockpile it; instead, maybe get two. Old glue just isn't as sticky as fresh new glue. Also, don't use just any old glue, like Elmer's or Super Glue! You want to make sure your glue is hypoallergenic so as not to harm your skin or eyes.

Funny story: At one point, I thought it was a great idea to wear triple eyelashes, which involves wearing three rows of lashes. Women would comment, "I love those eyelashes," while men would say to me, "Why are you wearing those eyelashes?" I decided I'd stick with single lashes!

TIPS

- Whether you are familiar with wearing makeup or want to try something new, I highly recommend you make an appointment with a professional makeup artist. Many of these consultations are free or low-cost. They can teach you how to apply your makeup and make recommendations on what makeup might work best for you.

- Look for smudge-proof, waterproof, or sweat-proof cosmetics.
- Choose lipsticks that stay on for 24 hours.
- There are eyebrow products on the market that have multiple tips that provide a more feathered natural brow look.
- Some people have fake eyebrows, which are little hairs sewn together on a silicone strip. Personally, these are not my favorite as they always look to me like they belong on Groucho Marx.

From the start of applying my makeup to the finish, it takes me about 10 minutes. However, at the beginning, it can take over an hour. Like I said previously, be patient!

CHAPTER 10

HOW TO LIVE YOUR BEST LIFE WITH OR WITHOUT HAIR

The loss of hair can lead to a loss of personal identity, self-esteem, and even social isolation. Understanding the psychological impact of hair loss can help people cope with their emotions and find ways to embrace their physical appearance. Grief and loss are emotions that are commonly associated with hair loss, especially in women.

The seven stages of grief explain the process people go through when they experience a significant loss. Elisabeth Kubler-Ross, in her book, *On Death and Dying*, first introduced the initial five stages of grief, which addresses the emotions and coping mechanisms of terminally ill patients. However, today, the seven stages of grief and loss are widely recognized and address much more than the process of dying. The model has been widely accepted as a way to understand and manage all kinds of loss, which could be the death of a loved one, a relationship breakdown, or losing your hair because of a medical condition or aging.

Stage 1: Shock and Denial

The first stage of grief is shock and denial. When people experience a significant loss, the first reaction is usually shock and disbelief. They struggle to accept the reality of the situation and their coping mechanism is to deny that it has happened. This is a way of protecting themselves from the harsh reality of their loss.

Stage 2: Pain and Guilt

The second stage of grief is pain and guilt. As reality begins to sink in, people start to feel intense emotions such as pain, sadness, and regret. They may also feel guilty about what they could have done differently to prevent the loss. This is a difficult stage, and people may experience depression and anxiety.

Stage 3: Anger and Bargaining

The third stage of grief is anger and bargaining. People in this stage often feel angry about the situation, and they may lash out at others or blame themselves. They may also try to make deals with a higher power or even the person they lost in an attempt to change the outcome.

Stage 4: Depression

The fourth stage of grief is depression. This stage is characterized by deep feelings of sadness, and the person may become withdrawn and isolated. They will spend a lot of time reflecting on their loss and the impact it has had on their life.

Stage 5: The Upward Turn

The fifth stage of grief is the upward turn. After spending a considerable amount of time in depression, people will begin to feel a little better. They start to see a light at the end of the tunnel, and life once again seems hopeful.

Stage 6: Reconstruction and Working Through

The sixth stage of grief is reconstruction and working through it. People in this stage begin to take steps to rebuild their life. This could mean seeking therapy, returning to work, or reconnecting with friends and family.

Stage 7: Acceptance and Hope

The seventh stage of grief is acceptance and hope. People that have made it to this stage have reached a point where they can begin to accept their loss. They feel a renewed sense of hope for their future and start to see the possibility of moving on, even though they may still be grieving.

My Thoughts on Grief and Loss Regarding Hair Loss

I believe there is an eighth stage of grief and loss – **This Is Who I Am.** In today's world, women being bald is no longer a stigma like it used to be. I love empowered women like Jada Pinkett Smith and others who are bold and proud of who they are. There is a popular female bodybuilder with alopecia who competes in all of her competitions without hair. It gives her body a sleek look that others don't have. It's so inspiring to me to see how far we've come from when I was a little girl growing up dealing with alopecia.

I simply love the idea that one step beyond acceptance is, "This is who I am. Isn't it wonderful?" It is so empowering for women.

Tanya has been a customer for almost 15 years. This is her story:
Tanya is an entrepreneur and powerful business owner in Seattle who has been dealing with hair loss most of her adult life. The first thing I remember about her is her humorous approach to hair loss. We recently had dinner with another hair-loss friend, and it was nonstop laughter. We told stories from our childhood, giving them a humorous spin. Covering painful memories with a funny story is one way to deal with them. At one point, Tanya got serious and reminded me of the seven stages of grief. The two of us are in Stage 7 – Acceptance, but that does not mean we skipped the previous six.

Carolyn B: A customer for over 20 years
Carolyn lost her hair at the age of 15. Like many of us, she was at a loss to understand what was happening. Carolyn was raised by her grandmother, and in those days, such things were not discussed. You know: If you don't talk about it, it's not actually happening. So, no family for support. Doctors did not have the answers either, so she was left to fend for herself. She felt so alone and endured nasty remarks and ridicule from other children, which hurt so much as a child and still stung as an adult. It took a few more years for all her hair to fall out during college. All she wanted was to be normal and not think something was wrong with her. One of her most horrific memories was when she was working as an aide. She tripped and fell, and her wig went flying. She did what many of us would have done: She retrieved her hair and ran into a back room, locking the door behind her. Her coworkers had to talk her out. It stung.

The loss of hair was bad enough, but one day, she lost her lashes and brows as well. Looking in the mirror each day only exacerbated her trauma.

One day, she took a look and declared: This is the new me. Get used to it, girl. You know it.

Carolyn fell in love, but she never talked about her hair loss with the man who eventually became her spouse. Can you imagine being married and not discussing the elephant in the room? This marriage soon failed, but another one was on the way. By the second marriage, her attitude had changed, and her second husband loved her for exactly who she was – hair or no hair. He was the love of her life.

As a spiritual person, Carolyn made a plea to God: it was okay to take her hair, but please, please, do not take it from her children or grandchildren. As a successful retired woman, she has now learned to love herself, hold her head high, and be exactly who she is. She is worthy and valuable, and her hair does not define her.

Now, she adorns herself with makeup and big earrings: NO HAIR at all. She says to hang in there, ladies, and be yourself. Others will love you for the beautiful bald person you are.

While I was writing this, Martha Stewart was on the cover of *Sports Illustrated*. She is someone who isn't afraid of change and ongoing transformation. Did I mention she is 81 and now a swimsuit model? My advice is that you've got to keep changing. If you get stuck in the ways you've always done things, you will age yourself.

I encourage you to take a chance and try a new look. It doesn't have to be a totally different look; rather, subtle highlights in your hair, a longer style or trying something trendy like having darker roots.

CHAPTER 11

SHARING THE LOVE

Hair care isn't half as tough as self-care. It's time to regain self-esteem and learn to love yourself. You are not your hair.

I find the most rewarding way to deal with my loss is to help others who are just starting the journey. Volunteer your time to mentor others by calling one of the support groups. Get on an outreach phone tree to mentor others who are in breakdown. Share with them your valuable experiences and words of wisdom.

I have been in the hair replacement business for over 40 years and speak to at least 10 women, men, and children per day. I learn something new each day for myself and others. I am here to be of support for all hair loss thrivers, and they are my teachers. Reach out and demonstrate that you are more than just your hair. You survive and thrive each day, with or without your hair.

The Birth of Locks of Love

I am thrilled for the young children who receive Locks of Love wigs.

By then, simply making it from day to day was an emotional balancing act. Despite a condition that had upended my life and self-confidence, I did not receive much family support or nurturing as a child, so I had to go outside my family network to find solace. When my hair began to fall out, my best friend, Kathy, was the most supportive influence in my life. She always stuck up for me and even got into a fistfight with one of the boys who took every possible opportunity to call me "baldy." And when my parents refused to acknowledge my need for a wig, Kathy helped me fund – and find – my first wig.

Kathy's help didn't stop there. One day about 40 years ago, she announced that she was growing her hair so that I could create a custom wig for myself. I didn't quite grasp the concept at the time, but over the months, as her hair got longer and longer, the act of love she was offering became increasingly apparent. When her hair finally got so long that it was driving her crazy, she announced that it was time to chop it off. We scheduled a styling appointment, with a photographer on hand to document the haircutting.

Making a Difference – Helping Kids With Locks of Love Charity

Little did we know that this would prove to be the first of many such events. That act of generosity prompted us to found Locks of Love, a charity that has since provided natural hairpieces to thousands of financially disadvantaged children all over the world suffering from hair loss.

Self-esteem is vital to all of us, but it's critical to kids and young adults. Over the years, I've watched faces change when I put hairpieces on heads. Those kids not only brighten up, they stand up! Young women who feel bad about themselves have the worst posture in the world. When they first come in to see me, their shoulders are rounded, and they look at the floor instead of up at me. But after I put a fabulous head of hair on their head, they walk out tall and bouncing, their hair flying.

I saw that renewed bounce again and again with Locks of Love: first during the 10 years that Kathy and I gave away hairpieces to children before filing for nonprofit status, then in the years that followed, as the organization garnered global fame. Thanks to media attention, children who were unable to afford natural hair wigs began sending in applications by the hundreds, and girls from all over the world began sending us the ponytails they'd purposefully grown. Soon we outgrew our offices and had to schedule volunteers to handle the volume of phone calls and emails we received.

Reading the letters from the children who lovingly cut and donated their hair proved the most rewarding part of the Locks of Love program. Some came from girls as young as three. They wrote in crayon and drew pictures of little girls with bald heads. These letters often brought tears to our eyes.

Although I am no longer actively involved in the operations of Locks of Love, they continue to receive donations of hair, which they turn into wigs for children in need. And Kathy continues to remind me of how the idea for the charity arose. As I ran my hands through her hair one day, I said: "I wish I had your hair." She said, "You can."

I am proud of my best friend, Kathy Hale, for being the inspiration behind Locks of Love, and so thankful for the good work of the volunteers and the children all over the country who selflessly cut their hair to benefit others in need. Most of all, I am thrilled for the young children who receive these wigs. For more information about Locks of Love, visit www.locksoflove.org.

Giving Back

When running Locks of Love, people would contact me wanting to donate their hair for their mother's wig if she was going through chemotherapy. Often, these were males. I had to deliver the news that one wig typically takes about 10 to 12 ponytails to make. I would suggest that instead of donating a small amount of hair, they make a donation to Locks of Love in honor of their mother.

One day I received a phone call from Darrell Sutton, a reverend at a California prison. He told me, "I have an entire cell block of Indigenous people here who have long hair down to their butts. We have a new grooming code here in our prison that requires that everyone cut their hair. They refused because they felt it was a religious right to keep their hair long. We told them they could, but they would lose privileges typically granted to prisoners for good behavior. That's when they had a powwow and determined they would all vow to cut their hair if it would be used in the making of a wig for a Native American child."

I shared with the reverend that I would gladly take the hair and would send rubber bands and a pouch to place the hair in, along with proper postage to do so. Eventually, I received in the mail a bunch of boxes with three-foot-long gray braids. I couldn't help but wonder what Native American child would want gray braided hair. However, as per the reverend's request, I simply earmarked it for Native American clients. The reverend would call and say something like, "Okay, we are sheering cell block three and will be sending more boxes to you!" Such a joy to receive.

If You Can't Afford a Wig or Don't Want to Invest the Money

There are nonprofit organizations that provide wigs free of charge. As most people going through chemotherapy who experience hair loss have their hair start growing back about six months later, people often opt to donate their wigs to charities such as the American Cancer Society. Your local American Cancer Society will probably have a wig bank. You can also search the internet for nonprofits in your area that might be able to help you. It's always good to give back, so if you no longer need your wig, consider donating it to a good cause like the American Cancer Society.

My intention in writing this book is so you may from someone who not only lives life without hair but also is knowledgeable in the wig industry. I wanted to tell you and others who are experiencing my journey and those of others who were also willing to recount theirs for you. You are not alone but you are unique. Take pride in who you are, stand tall, and be all you want to be.

As I do my final proofread through the chapters, I hear my own voice saying the words. The amount of factual information I have gathered throughout the years always surprises me. Throughout my journey, I have visited wig factories in three different facilities in the United States and six different countries. Each visit enhanced my knowledge and understanding of wig-making.

In addition, I have done extensive research, including in medical textbooks, which gave me an understanding of the makeup of hair. I have worked one-on-one with thousands of hair loss clients over a 40-year span. Sharing my knowledge is like leaving a legacy. If you still have questions after reading this book, feel free to call me directly. Yes, I actually answer the phone personally. I am also available to assist you with your wig or Enhancement Hair™ purchase.

Thank you for allowing me to share my story with you. May your hair loss journey be a smooth one.

MEDICAL HAIR LOSS GUIDE

Your Guide to Everything Hair Loss

The average person has approximately 90,000 to 150,000 scalp hairs. Natural blondes tend to have the most hairs (averaging 140,000), while brunettes and redheads fall on the lower end of the normal scale (averaging 105,000 and 90,000 hairs, respectively).

All scalp hair continually cycles through a lengthy growth period followed by a short resting phase and then loss. During the growth period, which lasts two to six years, hair emerges from a follicle and lengthens by roughly half an inch a month. It then enters a resting phase, which lasts just two to three months. After the hair is lost, a new hair emerges from the same follicle within six months.

It is normal to lose 50 to 150 hairs per day. True hair loss, or alopecia, occurs when an excessive number of hairs are lost over a short period of time or when hairs are not replaced in a timely or fully healthy fashion.

Stages of Hair Growth

Our own hair grows in three stages. In the case of alopecia, this growth pattern is interrupted.

Anagen – Growing Stage

- Between 80 and 90 percent of a healthy individual's hair is in the anagen phase, that is, the time when the hair is actively growing. On average, an individual human scalp hair remains in the anagen phase for about 1,000 days, or almost three years. However, this phase can last as long as eight years. The amount of time a hair spends in the anagen phase controls how long the hair will grow.

Catagen – Resting Stage

- The catagen phase is a short period of transition between the anagen and telogen phases. This phase lasts only one to three weeks. The catagen phase involves a period of major cell death, and only a remnant of the hair follicle remains at the completion of this phase. However, near the end of the catagen stage, movement of the dermal papilla occurs, setting the stage for regrowth.

Telogen – Shedding Stage

- During this stage, between 50 and 150 scalp hairs are lost each day. During this phase, hairs are only anchored by friction between the club-shaped root and the follicle. The telogen phase lasts approximately two or three months, a resting phase before the growth phase returns.

There are many medical causes for true hair loss, including:

- Androgenetic alopecia, often called male or female pattern hair loss
- Alopecia areata

- Burns and scars
- Cancer and cancer treatments
- Diabetes
- Hormonal imbalances, pregnancy, and thyroid disease
- Infection
- Lupus
- Malnutrition, including iron deficiency
- Medications and medical treatments
- Stress, trichotillomania, and other illness

Androgenetic Alopecia

The most common type of hair loss for both men and women is androgenetic alopecia, more often called male or female pattern hair loss. In the United States alone, an estimated 50 million men and 30 million women are affected.

This type of hair loss seems to be directly linked to heredity, aging, and the presence and level of specific hormones. A genetic predisposition toward androgenetic alopecia can be inherited from either a mother or a father. To some extent, genes also seem to determine the speed, pattern, and amount of loss. About 20 percent of people with alopecia have other autoimmune conditions.

Androgenetic alopecia is not yet fully understood, but it is clear that the normal cycle of hair growth, loss, and replacement is interrupted as a person ages and hormones fluctuate. It seems that over time (in most cases, very gradually) the scalp hair follicles shrink in size, subsequently generating hair that is finer and finer and shorter and shorter. Some follicles eventually generate no hair at all, though most remain alive, so they may still be capable of hair growth.

Related thinning and balding can begin in the teens, twenties, or thirties, but it often begins later in life. An estimated 25 percent of men are affected by age 30, and more than twice that percentage are affected by age 60. Women are affected in fewer numbers, and they are most commonly affected after menopause.

The pattern of thinning and loss also differs substantially between women and men. Men often lose hair first at their temples and at the crown of their head, and this loss may progress to complete baldness. Generally, the earlier the onset, the more extensive the loss. Women usually experience more diffuse and more mild or moderate thinning; they rarely experience baldness.

There is no known cure for male and female pattern hair loss, and such loss is considered permanent. But medical treatments are available to help slow or stop, and in some cases temporarily reverse, the progression of hair loss. The U.S. Food and Drug Administration (FDA) has approved the use of minoxidil for both men and women. This drug is available in over-the-counter topical lotions that can be applied to the scalp to stimulate hair follicles. The FDA has also approved the use of the prescription pill finasteride for men.

Alopecia Areata

Alopecia areata is a highly unpredictable autoimmune skin disease that may lead to the loss of hair on the scalp and elsewhere on the body. This disease affects males and females of all ages and races, but it often begins in childhood. This disease affects approximately 2 percent of the population or about 4.5 million people in the United States alone.

The exact cause of alopecia areata is unknown. It is thought that a combination of genes predisposes certain people to this disease, and some trigger—or possibly the confluence of several things—sets the disease off. The immune system then mistakenly attacks hair follicles, which shrink in size, arresting visible hair production.

The first sign of alopecia areata is usually one or more small, round, smooth bald patches on the scalp. Thereafter, the pattern of hair loss is unpredictable: initial patches can regrow hair, and all evidence of the disease may disappear for years; patches of hair loss can appear and disappear repeatedly; or the disease can progress to total scalp hair loss (alopecia totalis) or complete body hair loss (alopecia universalis) for an extended period of time. It is important to remember that even if a person has had alopecia for years, their hair follicles still hold the possibility for growth.

Alopecia areata is not life-threatening, but the loss of hair does make affected individuals more vulnerable to germs, dust, and other foreign particles entering the eyes, nose, and ears, and affected skin has diminished protection from sun, wind, and cold. Individuals with alopecia areata may also have an increased risk for atopic dermatitis, asthma and allergies, and thyroid disease.

Current treatments for alopecia areata often include the use of topical sensitizers such as diphencyprone or squaric acid dibutyl ester and topical medications like minoxidil or anthralin. Corticosteroids may also be applied topically or taken in pill form or injected. Additionally, some physicians utilize ultraviolet light and alternative therapies.

A person's age at the onset of alopecia areata, his or her current age, and the length and extent of hair loss often determine what treatments might be effective. In general, the earlier, the longer, and the greater the hair loss, the less likely it is that treatments will be effective in stimulating regrowth. The presence of atopic dermatitis may also indicate that treatments are likely to be ineffective.

The search for a cure is ongoing.

Burns and Scars

Hair loss on tissue that is badly burned or scarred has long been thought to be permanent, but a recent discovery in the field of cell research brings hope that new skin and hair may someday be grown from adult stem cells.

Cell biologists at Howard Hughes Medical Institute and The Rockefeller University in New York have not only identified such stem cells deep in the hair follicles of mice; they have also managed to isolate these cells and multiply them in a laboratory. And, as reported in the September 3, 2004, issue of the scientific journal *Cell*, when they grafted these cells onto bald mice, they grew both skin and tufts of hair.

Cancer and Cancer Treatments

Cancer, cancer treatments, and the stress related to cancer can all cause hair loss.

Skin cancers can cause extensive and permanent hair loss on the scalp and elsewhere. Merkel cell cancer is one rare but aggressive form of skin cancer that sometimes develops in hair follicles themselves; it affects the very specialized neurosecretory Merkel cells, which seem to play a key role in hair growth.

Lymphoma cells can mass in the skin and destroy hair follicles. Cancers elsewhere in the body, including the breasts, lungs, liver, and kidneys, can also metastasize, spreading to the skin and destroying hair follicles. Once hair follicles are destroyed, hair loss is permanent.

Cancer can also cause hair loss indirectly via anemia, hormonal imbalances, or other illnesses that can cause hair loss. Even the general physical and emotional stresses that naturally accompany a cancer diagnosis and cancer treatment can cause such loss. Such hair loss is generally diffuse and temporary.

Chemotherapy often results in temporary hair loss, while radiation therapy can result in either temporary or permanent hair loss.

Chemotherapy drugs target fast-growing cancer cells and seek to stop their rapid division and proliferation. Fast-growing normal cells, most often hair follicles, blood cells, and cells lining the gastrointestinal tract may also be affected. As hair cells stop dividing, hair shafts thin and break off.

Some chemotherapy drugs (including methotrexate, cyclophosphamide, bleomycin, doxorubicin, mitomycin, cytarabine, vinblastine, and vincristine) seem more likely than other drugs to cause hair loss, and some seem more likely to affect scalp hair while others lead to more universal loss. But all chemotherapy-related hair loss is highly variable. Some people experience hair loss, and others do not, even when they are taking the same drugs at the same dosage.

Hair can be lost gradually or in clumps, and it can happen at any time, but it usually begins one to three weeks after the start of chemotherapy and then worsens after a month or two. Sometimes as much as 90 percent of scalp hair is lost.

While nothing can prevent or stem this loss, there is good news: Once chemotherapy is completed, the hair usually grows back in six months to one year. Sometimes it even begins to grow back prior to the completion of treatment. This regrown hair may be very fine, it may break easily, and it may differ in color and texture from the hair that was originally lost.

It is generally best for chemotherapy patients to plan in advance for some hair loss. If a wig is desired, they might seek to match their original hair color and texture before it is lost. Custom-made wigs and hair prosthetics take up to four months for production and delivery.

Radiation therapy generally causes loss only in the specific area being treated. The dosage of the radiation may determine whether this hair loss is temporary or permanent. As with chemotherapy, if hair returns, it may differ in color and texture from the original hair that was lost.

Diabetes

Diabetes may result in hair loss for a wide variety of reasons.

People with diabetes are very susceptible to skin problems, which often lead to hair loss. Some of these skin problems, like bacterial and fungal infections, affect many people, but diabetics get them more easily and more often. Other skin problems, like diabetic blisters, diabetic dermopathy, necrobiosis lipoidica diabeticorum, and eruptive xanthomatosis, primarily affect diabetics – most often on their extremities.

Because of poor blood circulation, diabetics heal more slowly and scar more often from injuries, cuts, and scrapes.

Diabetes can also lead to many other problems, like hormonal imbalances, kidney disease, and weight loss, which can also cause hair loss.

Hormonal Imbalances, Pregnancy, and Thyroid Disease

Hormonal changes and imbalances, no matter what the cause, often result in hair loss.

Androgenetic alopecia, the most common cause of hair loss, is tied to the presence and levels of certain androgen hormones, particularly testosterone, in men and women. Though the hair follicles maintain the possibility for growth, and certain therapies seem to temporarily slow, stop, or even reverse the loss, androgenetic alopecia is generally considered permanent.

Similarly, **ovarian overproduction of androgen** can result in hair loss in women. This condition may require hormonal therapy, and even after the underlying problem is treated, the hair loss may not improve.

Androgen therapy (including the use of testosterone and DHEA) to treat a low sex drive in women can also result in hair loss.

Polycystic ovary syndrome, which is usually initiated by high levels of luteinizing hormone, androgen, or estrogen, can cause hair loss in teenage girls and women.

Hair loss following pregnancy is tied to fluctuating levels of the hormone estrogen, and this hair loss is generally temporary. During pregnancy, women experience a rise in estrogen, and this causes more hairs than normal to remain in the active growth portion of the hair cycle.

(Hair loss during pregnancy is unusual and may be a sign of deficient vitamins and minerals.) After delivery, estrogen decreases, and more hairs enter the resting phase and are soon lost. Noticeable loss often begins two to three months after the pregnancy ends, it may progressively worsen for up to four months after pregnancy, and it may continue for six to twelve months.

Similarly, the use of **birth control pills**, which usually contain progestin and estrogen, can cause hair loss, particularly in women who have an inherited tendency for androgenetic alopecia. And when birth control pills are discontinued, hair loss similar to that following pregnancy may result. This loss often begins two to three months after the pills are discontinued, and it may continue for several months.

Diseases of the thyroid and pituitary glands, which regulate hormones, also often result in hair loss. If hormonal balance is restored, hair loss is often temporary, but it can be permanent.

An overactive thyroid (or *hyper*thyroid) generally causes hair to become fine and soft, and there can be scattered loss. An underactive thyroid (or *hypo*thyroid) causes hair to become coarse and dry, also potentially causing scattered loss. These thyroid problems can also result from Graves' disease, thyroid tumors, or abnormalities of the pituitary, the hypothalamus, the testes, or the ovaries.

The pituitary gland is located at the base of the brain, and it interacts with the thyroid in regulating hormones. Pituitary tumors can cause hair growth or loss, or both sequentially. Some pituitary tumors initially stimulate increased hormonal production, but as the tumor grows and as regular pituitary cells are suppressed or destroyed, fewer hormones are produced. Hair growth increases or decreases along with these hormonal fluctuations. Pituitary tumors are usually benign (noncancerous), and the general prognosis is good if they can be surgically removed, but hormonal imbalances may be permanent and may require hormone replacement therapy.

Infection

Several fungal and bacterial infections cause temporary hair loss.

Ringworm, a fungal infection that is highly contagious, most often affects children, but it can also affect adults, particularly diabetics, and others with compromised immune systems. It can infect the scalp or other parts of the body, including the groin and the feet. The first signs of this infection are small patches of scaling skin with a sharply defined, red edge or "ring" around them. These patches can spread, blister, and ooze, and hair in these areas is soon lost. This infection is easily treated with topical or oral antifungal medications.

Cutaneous candidiasis, another fungal infection, most often affects individuals who are obese or have compromised immune systems. Candida can infect skin anywhere on the body, but it most often occurs in warm, moist areas such as the armpits. Symptoms include intense itching, a skin lesion or rash, and infected pimple-like hair follicles (folliculitis). Candida is generally treated with topical antifungal medication, but a more systemic approach may be required for folliculitis.

Folliculitis of the scalp or skin is most often due to bacterial infection by staphylococcus germs. While such an infection can be very serious, it can now be treated with both oral and topical antibiotics. Folliculitis can recur and become chronic.

Lupus

Like diabetes, lupus, which is an autoimmune disease, may lead to hair loss for many different reasons.

Generalized hair loss is one symptom of systemic lupus erythematosus. Lupus flares can interrupt normal hair growth, leading to hair that is thin and breaks easily. The resulting loss is generally temporary and diffuse.

People with lupus are also very susceptible to skin diseases and infections, many of which can lead to hair loss. In addition to skin diseases and infections that affect other segments of the population, people with lupus may experience discoid lesions and sub-acute or acute cutaneous lesions. Discoid lesions, in particular, can result in scarring and discoloration, and localized permanent baldness. These lesions, which are initially coin-shaped areas of red, scaly, and thickened skin located most often on the scalp, are often the first sign of lupus. On a more positive note, the majority of people who get this "lupus of the skin" do not go on to develop full-blown systemic lupus erythematosus.

More indirectly, systemic lupus erythematosus can lead to kidney and blood diseases that also cause hair loss.

Hair loss may also result from some of the drugs used to treat lupus, particularly antineoplastics, corticosteroids, and immuno-suppressives.

Malnutrition and Anemia

Malnutrition, whether due to poor diet or eating disorders like anorexia and bulimia, often leads to hair loss. Seemingly healthy vegetarian diets that don't concentrate on providing enough protein can have the same result as can diets that don't provide adequate iron or zinc. Even physician-approved diets that lead to slow and healthy weight loss can result in some hair loss—usually three to six months after a loss of 15 pounds or more.

In an effort to conserve scarce protein resources, the body shifts hairs from the growth to the resting stage. The loss is gradual and diffuse and may not be noticed until nearly half of all hair is lost. This hair loss almost always reverses itself when an adequate diet is restored.

Medications and Medical Treatments

Many different medications and medical treatments can cause either temporary or permanent hair loss. Cancer treatments are notorious for this. Chemotherapy drugs, including antineoplastics like bleomycin and vinblastine, often cause temporary loss, while radiation therapy can cause either permanent or temporary loss, depending on the location and dose of the treatment.

Immunosuppressive medications, like methotrexate, which are used to treat autoimmune diseases like lupus and arthritis or to prevent the rejection of transplanted organs, also often cause temporary hair loss.

Other medicinal causes of what is usually just temporary hair loss include:

- The use or discontinued use of certain steroids and hormone regulators like birth control pills
- Psychiatric drugs used to treat depression and bipolar disease
- Drugs used to treat heart problems and high blood pressure
- Anticoagulants and blood thinners
- Potent skin and acne medications like isotretinoin
- Diet pills that contain amphetamines

- Some preventive vaccinations, particularly the hepatitis B vaccine, are also associated with hair loss. And hair loss can even be caused by too much of certain vitamins, particularly vitamin A.

Stress, Trichotillomania, and Other Illness

Over 30 specific diseases, including diabetes and lupus, as well as diseases of the liver, kidney, and thyroid, are known to cause permanent or long-term hair loss. However, hair loss can also result from general illness: A high fever or a bad case of flu can initiate loss that is noticeable in one to four months but usually reverses itself soon thereafter, and chronic illness can cause chronic loss. Hair loss also often occurs after surgery.

Basically, any undue stress, whether physical or emotional, can result in hair loss.

Trichotillomania, a psychological disorder that may be linked to stress, involves the compulsive pulling or twisting of hair, resulting in patchy or diffuse hair loss. This compulsion is thought to affect as much as 4 percent of the population, and it seems to affect females four times more often than males. This compulsion generally manifests itself before the age of 17 and is often limited to a period of a year or so. The earlier this compulsion appears and the sooner it is treated, the better the prognosis. Trichotillomania is not well understood, and some medical professionals believe that it is simply an ingrained bad habit, but it is sometimes treated with therapy and antidepressants.

JAK Inhibitors

They may cause hair loss as an unwanted side effect of treatment; some studies indicate this. They could result in temporary hair thinning or loss in some patients taking JAK inhibitors. Keep in mind that hair loss may not be an inevitable risk associated with JAK inhibitors; rather, its severity depends on several variables related to medication dosage and the genetic makeup of the person taking the medication.

New Treatment for Alopecia Areata Receives FDA Approval

On June 13, 2022, the U.S. Food and Drug Administration (FDA) approved Olumiant (baricitinib) for the treatment of severe alopecia areata in adults. This marks the first-ever approved treatment for the disease. Baricitinib is part of the class of drugs known as JAK inhibitors and is the first of several JAK inhibitors that have completed late-stage clinical trials for alopecia areata patients.

ADDITIONAL RESOURCES

Government Agencies

National Institutes of Health

(NIH) — an agency of the U.S. Department of Health and Human Services that serves as the steward of medical and behavioral research for the nation. Search its website, nih.gov, particularly the MedlinePlus database maintained by the NIH's National Library of Medicine, to learn the very latest research regarding all types of medical hair loss.

Professional Societies

American Academy of Dermatology

(AAD) — the largest dermatologic association representing virtually all dermatologists in the United States. Through its website, aad.org, you can locate a dermatologist, read the latest hair loss research, and access patient brochures.

American Hair Loss Council

(AHLC) — a nonprofit organization of hair loss specialists. Its website, ahlc.org, discusses primary types of hair loss, myths regarding the

cause, and surgical and nonsurgical treatments. It also offers referrals to local hair specialists, though it does not endorse individuals or businesses.

Primary Health Organizations

American Cancer Society

(ACS) — a nationwide, community-based voluntary health organization dedicated to eliminating cancer as a major health problem by preventing cancer, saving lives, and diminishing suffering from cancer, through research, education, advocacy, and service. Its informative and accessible website, cancer.org, offers cancer facts and figures, the latest related medical news, and a listing of local and national activities, as well as strong support for patients and their families.

American Diabetes Association

(ADA) — a national nonprofit health organization providing diabetes research, information, and advocacy in order to prevent and cure diabetes and to improve the lives of all people affected by diabetes. Its website, diabetes.org, offers a wealth of information on this disease, including information on diabetes-related skin problems and hair loss. It also discusses current treatments and progress in research, it hosts a multitude of message boards, and it lists community programs and events.

The Lupus Foundation of America

(LFA) — a national nonprofit volunteer health organization dedicated to finding the cause and cure for lupus. Research, education, and patient services are at the heart of its many programs; it seeks to improve the diagnosis and treatment of lupus, support individuals and families affected by the disease, and increase awareness of lupus

among health professionals and the public. Its website, lupus.org, offers a wealth of information on lupus-related hair loss.

National Alopecia Areata Foundation

(NAAF) — an international nonprofit community-based health organization that strives to support research to find a cure or acceptable treatment for alopecia areata, to support those affected by this disease, and to educate the public about this disease. In addition to a wealth of information, its website, naaf.org, offers access to very active online message boards for both children and adults, as well as to its new marketplace of hair loss products. You can also order a free video for children with hair loss and a special packet of information on how to get your insurance company to reimburse you for the purchase of a medical hair prosthesis.

ABOUT THE AUTHOR

Peggy Knight Wigs is the leading provider of hair prostheses for medical hair loss. Peggy's personal experience with hair loss is her inspiration and motivation. It is the foundation for her goals and actions today and every day. As a teenager, Peggy developed alopecia areata, an autoimmune disease that causes hair loss and has no known cause or cure. By age 21, she had lost all of her hair. She was then working in a high-visibility position as a flight attendant and struggled to maintain her self-esteem in the face of society's expectations. At the time, there was little understanding of, and little compassion for, individuals experiencing hair loss or thinning because of alopecia areata or other medical causes (such as stress, chemotherapy, or scars). The marketplace offered little solace: acceptable wig and hairpiece products were almost impossible to locate. In an effort to help herself and others, Knight founded an image institute in 1982. This institute, located in San Francisco, California, focused on helping women regain their self-esteem and return to a normal, active lifestyle after experiencing changes in their physical appearance due to alopecia areata, other hair loss diseases, burns, or cancer treatments. The institute also nurtured the development of the high-quality hairpieces and wigs now available through Peggy Knight Wigs. Today, as founder and president of Peggy Knight Wigs, Peggy oversees the research and development of a full product line of wigs and custom hairpieces created specifically for girls, teens, and women with medical hair loss.

"I am committed to creating hair prostheses that enable every-one experiencing hair loss to lead a normal life – to walk in the wind or play sports without worry," Peggy says. In her quest to help people through hair loss, Peggy Knight has been designing her signature wigs for over 40 years. She is a world-renowned expert on the subject of hair loss in women and has appeared on many programs and in many publications.

Peggy's concepts have been featured on:

☐ CNN
☐ The Oprah Winfrey Show
☐ 20/20
☐ The New Maury Povich Show
☐ Dermatology Nurses
☐ Nursing Magazine
☐ Hair & Beauty News
☐ Modern Salon
☐ Beauty Education
☐ American Salon
☐ Entrepreneurial Woman
☐ San Francisco Chronicle
☐ Oakland Tribune
☐ Los Angeles Times
☐ Gayle King Show
☐ People Magazine
☐ Extra
☐ Today Show
☐ Cosmopolitan Magazine
☐ Hour Magazine
☐ Dr. Dean Edell
☐ Telemundo Television

☐ Nickelodeon Television

☐ The Courage to Give

☐ The Tyra Banks Show

Of course, I'm equally proud of the work I've done through Peggy Knight Wigs to help young girls, teens, and women of all ages to live happy, normal lives despite the loss of their hair. For more information about Peggy Knight Wigs, please feel invited to look around the www.peggyknight.com site or just contact us.

You can reach us by phone at (415) 877-7004 or by email at peggy@peggyknight.com

ACKNOWLEDGEMENTS

I wish to acknowledge Ashley Siegel, founder of the National Alopecia Areata Foundation, for opening my eyes and making me believe in myself – with or without hair.